Ministry and the Mystical Path: Formation Guide for Lay Ministers

BARBARA HUGHES

Ed, Thanks for your interest. Hope you enjoy! Barbara Hughes

National Catholic Educational Association

The National Catholic Educational Association
1005 North Glebe Road, Suite 525
Arlington, VA 22201
800.711.6232 • www.ncea.org

Second Printing 2014
Part No.: REL-24-1435
ISBN: 1-55833-437-8

TABLE OF CONTENTS

PART II – THE NIGHT OF THE SENSES

PART III - THE NIGHT OF THE SPIRIT

FOREWORD

Midway in the Gospel of Mark, we discover an amazing switch in Jesus' public ministry. Up to this point the Evangelist describes in his first eight chapters Jesus' almost feverish activity in Galilee establishing the Kingdom of God. He calls disciples to join him in proclaiming the Good News of salvation, and he begins forming them into a community. He frees persons from diabolic possession. He heals the sick. He teaches eager crowds about the mystery of the Kingdom of God. He calms the stormy Sea of Galilee, saving his terrified disciples from perishing. He feeds multitudes by miraculously multiplying a few loaves and fish.

And then suddenly, at Caesarea Phillipi, everything changes. Jesus tells His disciples that He must "suffer greatly and be rejected by the elders, the chief priests, and the scribes, and be killed, and rise after three days"(Mk 8:31). As popular and successful as He was, Jesus apparently now realizes that His many efforts in Galilee are not succeeding in establishing God's reign in people's hearts. His disciples do not understand Him, the crowds misinterpret His marvelous words and deeds, and the Pharisees want to destroy Him. Jesus abruptly leaves Galilee and Mark devotes the last eight chapters of his narrative to the Teacher's journey to Jerusalem and His ministry in the city where His prophecy of death and resurrection is fulfilled. He must now complete his Galilean ministry in Jerusalem. There, in obedience to His Father's mysterious will, Jesus becomes the Lamb sacrificed for the people's salvation. In Jerusalem, where the paschal lamb is slaughtered, Jesus fulfills the Paschal Mystery, opening God's kingdom to all people.

A sure moment of grace in our lives as pastoral ministers, whether ordained or lay, comes when we finally understand that ministry involves not only sharing Jesus' active ministry in Galilee, but also His paschal ministry in Jerusalem. "Whoever wishes to come after me must deny himself, take up his cross, and follow me. For whoever wishes to save his life will lose it, but whoever loses his life for my sake and that of the gospel will save it."(Mk 8:34 - 35). Losing our life for Jesus and the Gospel means not only teaching, healing, preaching, and building community in His name, but also sharing daily in His passion, death, and resurrection. It means continually dying to our own self so that Jesus may live and minister in us through the Holy Spirit. Effective ministry depends not solely on the success of our external activity, but more fundamentally on our dying and rising interiorly with Jesus Christ, which alone brings forward the Kingdom of God.

No one understood this better than St. John of the Cross. He maintains in his *The Ascent of Mount Carmel* that Jesus' greatest act of ministry was his self-emptying death on the cross. Here Jesus "accomplished the most marvelous work of his whole life, surpassing all the works and deeds and miracles that he had ever performed on earth or in heaven. That is, he brought about the reconciliation and union of the human race with God through grace." [1] John further reminds those who participate in Jesus' ministry of reconciling the human family with God that "their union with God and the greatness of the work they accomplish will be measured by the annihilation of themselves for God in the sensory and spiritual parts of their souls."[2] This total death to self, both in sense and in spirit, is required both for union with God and for effective ministry.

John, of course, wrote primarily for contemplatives, describing the mystical path of self-emptying leading to union with and transformation in God. But his writings can equally apply to those in active pastoral ministry who may not think of themselves as called to contemplation. Their effectiveness as ministers, too, requires union with and transformation of their lives in God. John knew this from personal experience. His preaching and sacramental ministry, his spiritual guidance of numerous persons, his writing, and his administrative responsibilities in the first years of St. Teresa of Avila's reform of the Carmelite order once led him to remark, "the Lord gives us so much to do these days that we can hardly keep up with it all."[3] But busy as he was, prayer and spiritual practice always remained his priorities. He understood that the purification of his mind and heart, of his pride and fears, so necessary for union with God, also made him a more fit instrument of Jesus' redemptive and reconciling mission. He observed that when, through "contemplative purgation or nakedness and poverty of spirit (which are all about the same)," he departed from "my low manner of understanding, and my feeble way of loving, and my poor and limited method of finding satisfaction in God," he then "went out from my human operation and way of acting to God's operation and way of acting."[4] Those in active ministry, like those in the contemplative life, will find in John's writings a tested and secure way to die to their limited human ways of behaving in order to act as God acts.

Admittedly, John is not easy reading. His theology, psychology, spirituality, and language often seem beyond the modern Christian reader. Barbara Hughes has done a great service to lay ministers in today's church, both volunteers and professionals, by translating John's spiritual teachings into language they can readily understand. Drawing on her own extensive experience as wife, mother, psychiatric nurse, and lay minister for many years and now as a spiritual director and leader of retreats and workshops for lay ministers, Barbara shows how John's teaching for contemplatives applies equally to ministers. She shows, for example, that ministry's inevitable disillusionments, hardships, and suffering can be, like the dark night of contemplatives, God's way of purifying the motivation of ministers, deepening their faith, and secretly communicating to their souls. Although apparently dissimilar in the beginning, the contemplative's way and the minister's way share the same inner dynamics, leading both eventually to the total surrender of self for the sake of God's kingdom.

Convinced that spiritual formation is the greatest current need for the growing number of laity assuming responsibility for pastoral leadership in the Church in the United States, Barbara offers her book as a "spiritual guide for lay ministers." A Carmelite secular herself, she draws on Carmel's rich spiritual heritage, primarily the teachings of St. John of the Cross, as well as modern spiritual masters such as Thomas Merton and Mother Teresa of Calcutta, to show how the way of the mystics can also be a fruitful spiritual path for ministers. Ministers who follow her careful guidance will find themselves led deeper into the death and resurrection of Jesus Christ, the Paschal Mystery that is the life of Christian mystics and the heart of lay pastoral ministry.

Kevin Culligan, O.C.D.
Institute of Carmelite Studies
Feast of All Saints, 2008

PREFACE

Since Vatican Council II, Catholic lay women and men have answered the Baptismal call to become co-workers in the vineyard of the Lord. Indeed, Catholics heard the message in *The Dogmatic Constitution on the Church (Lumen Gentium)*, no. 40, "that all Christians in whatever state or walk of life are called to the fullness of Christian life and to the perfection of charity, and this holiness is conducive to a more human way of living even in society here on earth." Further, they heeded Pope Paul VI's words in *On Evangelization in the Modern World (Evangelii Nuntiandi)*, no. 73, that "[t]he laity can also feel called, or in fact be called, to cooperate with their pastors in the service of the ecclesial community, for the sake of its growth and life. This can be done through the exercise of different kinds of ministries according to the grace and charisms which the Lord has been pleased to bestow on them."

The number of lay ecclesial ministers now number in excess of 30,000 (DeLambo, 2008). Laity clearly got the message: God calls; we respond. In parishes, hospitals and educational institutions, lay Catholics have voted with their feet to become actively involved on behalf of the gospel in unprecedented numbers. The paths to ministry are varied but all paths stem from a singular love of God and willingness to stake one's life on what is eternally important and meaningful.

Ministry and the Mystical Path: A Spiritual Formation Guide for Lay Ministers is sure to speak to the hearts of all these laity who have answered the baptismal call to be co-workers in the vineyard of the Lord. Written by a lay minister who knows of what she speaks and writes, Barbara Hughes artfully translates the work of spiritual masters such as St. John of the Cross and St. Teresa of Avila into modern parlance. Weaving together the spiritual journey in relation to experience in lay ministry, she describes the mystical path in accessible and practical ways that illuminates the path for all those who labor as co-workers and collaborators on behalf of the gospel.

Recognizing that lay ministers in the catechetical and educational fields need to be attentive to their spiritual growth and development as well as professional and academic growth, the Department of Religious Education has directed more of its resources and services for members to address this need. *Ministry and the Mystical Path* is aimed at this audience as well as all lay ministers who may find it helpful.

I thank Barbara Hughes for sharing this book with us in print and taking the message to our members as a facilitator for the Spiritual Deepening Day with the National Association of Parish Catechetical Directors (NPCD) Convocation 2009 in Anaheim, California. Her practical and well-grounded approach with thoughtful reflection questions make this a book that can keep on giving beyond the first read.

I am especially grateful to the staff in the Department of Religious Education who assisted me in the production process: Dr. Robert Brancatelli, Christina Gergits, Jessica McMiller and NCEA designer, Jean Philippe Laplagne. Many hands make work light and this work has been a labor of love. May it be a blessing to all who read it.

Diana Dudoit Raiche
Executive Director
Department of Religious Education

ACKNOWLEDGEMENTS

I would like to thank my longtime friend and mentor, Father Kevin Culligan, O.C.D. for his encouragement and careful reading of my work, and evaluation of its accuracy in interpreting the teachings of Carmelite spirituality, specifically the teachings of St. John of the Cross and St. Teresa of Avila. I also owe a debt of gratitude to Vinita Hampton Wright for encouraging me to undertake this work.

I dedicate this book to my husband Mike for his unwavering love and support.

INTRODUCTION

Since the Second Vatican Council, the role of the laity within the Church community continues to be defined. With renewed emphasis on the Baptismal call for all Catholics to share their gifts, many lay men and women have come of age, placing their charisms in service to the Church. Today, they hold pastoral positions that were once open only to clergy or religious. Equipped with graduate degrees, they serve as educators, catechetical leaders, chaplains and administrators of Catholic institutions. In response to a virtual explosion of professional men and women embracing the call to serve, the United States Conference of Catholic Bishops has established subcommittees for research and has published documents clarifying the scope and phenomenon of lay ecclesial ministry. As more and more people continue to fill staff positions on the parish and diocesan level, one thing is clear: for ministers to grow in holiness, the blending of spiritual principles with apostolic practice is imperative.

Perseverance and effective ministry require more than education and a willing heart. Ecclesial ministers who embrace the Baptismal mandate to further the Kingdom of God without a strong spiritual foundation frequently become victims of human frailty, their own and that of others. As a result, many well-intentioned lay ministers, both professional and volunteer, get caught in the downward spiral of disillusionment and burnout. But that need not be the case if ministers take advantage of the rich heritage that is theirs. The life and the teachings of Jesus together with the wisdom and guidance of the saints who have dedicated their lives to building the Kingdom have much to offer.

This point came clear to me during a dream I had following on the heels of a very intensive year in parish ministry. I dreamt that after years of living in my house, I discovered, much to my surprise, that my home had a basement. In my excitement I visited family and friends to share the good news but when I arrived, each was eager to show me the basement they had just discovered in their own home. Although everyone had lived in their house for a number of years, no one knew it had a basement. As I went from one home to another, I realized that the basements shared something in common. They all had earthen floors and brick walls and every basement was filled with children who were laughing and playing. Discovering the basements proved to be a deep source of joy, so much so that even people who did not have a basement wanted one and were eager to begin the excavation process.

Since then I have thought a lot about that dream. I have come to realize that the basements represent God who had been there all along. The brick walls were the people and experiences that form us along the way. But it was more than just the people who physically accompanied us on the journey that formed us. The bricks represented the mystics and saints and those on whose shoulders we stand - apostles and prophets, mentors and martyrs whose blood ran so that we could inherit the law of love that Jesus left the world. And in-between each brick was grace, the mortar that holds it all together.

Like the homeowners in the dream who discovered a basement, those who descend into the depths of their hearts discover God on a profound and intimate level. They encounter the source of their joy and, much like children who laugh and play, they discover their yoke is easy and their burden light. All they have to do is open the door and God is there, bearing the weight of the burdens they thought were theirs. I find a wonderful parallel between the message in this dream and ministry.

It is easy to get caught up in the doing of ministry. The open ended nature of the work can quickly engulf any well-intentioned person. A combination of mission, personal passion and guilt can overtake the unsuspecting minister until ministry begins to feel more like a chasm than a charism.

When hearts and minds are pre-occupied, filled with plans and activities, worries and deadlines, then the minister's work, as good as it may be, is like a house whose upstairs has been cleaned and decorated but whose basement has been ignored. Cracks in the foundation creep in and if left unattended, the walls begin to shift and rodents and insects find a home. When a storm comes, flood waters seep in and when they recede, a layer of sludge is left behind. If the basement remains unexamined and the mortar is not reinforced, the foundation weakens and the house eventually crumbles. And so it is with ministry. When ministers become so preoccupied with the task at hand that they lose sight of the ground on Whom their work stands, their spiritual well-being is threatened.

No one in the active apostolate would dispute the fact that unless the Lord builds a house, the laborer's work is in vain. Yet knowing this and living it are quite different. The one has to do with knowledge; the other requires a purposeful descent into the center of the minister's being. Typically, the descent takes place in incremental stages, not unlike the deepening stages of prayer. The process requires grace, continued effort and ongoing commitment. Ministers who actively seek to grow more deeply in love with God are strengthened during times of difficulty and as a result, their apostolate remains centered in God.

Paradoxically, many in lay ministry place their spiritual health at risk for the sake of the people they serve. When generous hearts give without taking time to receive from the One who calls them, they are in danger of running on empty. The culprits appear innocent enough, but the effects can be devastating. A deep sense of responsibility toward God and church together with misplaced feelings of inadequacy can turn unsuspecting ministers into work-alcoholics. Too often they convince themselves that their work is their prayer. But ministry can never be a substitute for prayer. Unless ministry is rooted in the minister's relationship with God, and fostered through prayer, it is like a house built on sandy soil that cannot support its foundation. And without a foundation, the house will be swept away when under siege from stress or the day-to-day challenges that are part of ministry.

A closer analysis reveals that when problems arise, responsible people look for solutions. Since responsible people tend to be very busy people, a quick fix is usually more appealing than one that requires time and ongoing effort. As a result, a one hour presentation, a workshop or lunch with a colleague is often used to prop up sagging spirits. While these can be helpful, more is needed. Unfortunately, many people in ministry labor under the illusion that they cannot afford time away from work. But the truth is: anyone who is serious about ministry cannot afford not to take the time. Ministry is not just about what we do, it is about who we are.

But what exactly do we mean when we talk about lay ministry? Many use the term ministry to describe works of service in the Church or the world, performed by the Baptized in the name of Christ. Others believe that every person is called to ministry since we are created in the image and likeness of God and that Baptism is simply a celebration of that call. In *Co-Workers in the Vineyard of the Lord,* the United States Conference of Catholic Bishops points out that as members of the Body of Christ, all the Baptized are equipped with gifts and graces to build up the Church and to contribute to the sanctification of the world. But the Bishop's Conference chose the term "lay ecclesial ministers" to describe lay persons who perform a service within the Church community.

Since all who are Baptized share in Christ's mission, lay ministry is rooted in relationship. Intrinsic to our understanding of ministry is the fact that it is not just about relationships with the people we serve. Lay ministry is about the lay minister's relationship with God.

The definitions for ministry offered above may seem broad but the more spiritually integrated a person's life becomes, the more every act done in the name of Jesus, for the glory of God, can rightly be called lay ministry. When the vocation to spread the Good News of Jesus Christ through word and example is taken seriously, Christians realize that all are called to serve. The faces of ministry are as varied as the people who are called. From ordained minister to mother, from catechist to cashier, all could be regarded as lay ministers.

However, for the purpose of this book, I have narrowed the discussion of ministry to works that are done specifically for or in the name of the Church. This is not to lessen the importance of lay ministry as a Christian vocation for all who are Baptized, but to address the occupational hazards of those who labor in the ecclesial vineyard. Its aim is to address the unique set of challenges that confront lay ecclesial ministers, both professionals and volunteers.

Catechists, R.C.I.A. sponsors, and the cadre of deeply committed volunteers who are co-workers in the vineyard can rightly be called lay ecclesial ministers. And it has been my experience that the same dangers exist for both professionals and volunteers.

As a spiritual director and retreat facilitator, I spend hours listening to the joys and heartaches of those who place furthering the Kingdom of God high on their list of priorities. But when ministry becomes an endless series of tasks to accomplish or projects to manage, working for the Church is reduced to just another job. When this happens, everyone suffers.

Whether a paid professional or a volunteer, lay ecclesial ministers need a support system. In order to stand secure in the face of storms, they need a firm foundation built on solid ground and Jesus Christ is the ground upon which the active apostolate must stand. Those called to the active apostolate need one another and they need those who have traveled the road before them. They are the bricks that form the foundation. But vigilance and discernment are also important.

When is it time to move on? How do you know if you are being called in another direction or if you are simply trying to escape? These are valid questions but in the absence of a life of prayer, how will you discern where God is leading you?

Perhaps you are new to ministry, or maybe you have been toiling for years. Whatever your role, wherever you may be on the journey, my hope is that ministers, both professionals and volunteers, will find this offering a useful tool. I ask that you read it prayerfully and spend time with the questions at the end of each chapter.

Lastly, this book has been written as a tribute to the many ordinary men and women, novice and veteran who long for the Kingdom of God with all their heart. My hope is that those who read it will discover their inner beauty as a child of God and in so doing will remain steadfast in a life of service as they fall more deeply in love with God each day.

ABBREVIATIONS

All Scripture quotations are taken from the *New American Bible – The Catholic Study Bible* (© 1990, Oxford University Press, Inc.)

Unless otherwise noted, all quotations from St. John of the Cross are taken from *The Collected Works of St. John of the Cross,* translated by Kieran Kavanaugh and Otolio Rodriguez (Washington, DC: ICS Publications, 1979). The following abbreviations have been used to cite his work.

AMC = *Ascent of Mount Carmel*
SC = *Spiritual Canticle*
DN = *Dark Night*

All quotations from St. Teresa of Avila are taken from Vol. II of *The Collected Works of St. Teresa of Avila,* translated by Kieran Kavanaugh and Otolio Rodriguez (Washington, DC: ISC Publications, 1980). The following abbreviations have been used to cite her work.

IC = *Interior Castle*
WP = *The Way of Perfection*

Part I

From Romance to Disillusionment

CHAPTER I

CALLED TO RELATIONSHIP

DUAL PATHS

So...how is your prayer life? The answer to the question may reveal more about the quality of your ministry than you know. Unlike a performance review, only you can evaluate the quality of your ministry. Quality is all encompassing. It takes into account your interior disposition, motivation and your relationship with God. Performance simply evaluates your skill and work ethic. The former offers a view from within, the latter is about functionality. While performance measures capability, quality is about intentionality and the graced path of transformation. Consequently, the quality of your ministry is directly proportionate to the quality of your prayer life. And both are reliable indicators of the depth of your relationship with God.

While some regard active ministry as being at odds with the contemplative path, both paths lead to union with God, when the focus is God. And while not all are called to the religious or ordained life, all are called to union.

During His last discourse Jesus prayed, "As you Father are in me and I in you, that they also may be in us, that the world may believe that you sent me" (Jn 17:21). When He was preparing His disciples for ministry in the world, Jesus, addressing the Father said, "As you sent me into the world, so I sent them into the world. And I consecrate myself for them, so that they also may be consecrated in truth" (Jn 17:18-19).

Before sending His disciples into the world, Jesus prayed that they would not be owned by the world. But Jesus also knew that the dangers in ministry were not merely external. He was well acquainted with the dynamics of human behavior and understood that the enemy also lurks within. The struggle for mastery over the human spirit by the demons within is present in even the most well intentioned people. The struggle is real and the most effective weapon is a deep and profound prayer life. Jesus' life gave witness to this truth. He began His ministry with a sojourn into the desert to fast and pray, and we know from Scripture that He often rose early to pray. There were times when He spent the entire night in prayer. Both personal and communal prayer were integral to Jesus' public ministry, and that alone should convince ministers about the importance of prayer.

Prayer and ministry cannot be separated. Rather than one path hindering the other, the two paths nurture one another. Through the ages, those who have devoted their lives to prayer have contributed much to building the Kingdom of God. This suggests that contemplatives have much to teach us about both prayer and ministry. Their lives were fruitful because they were fully conscious of their call to union with the Triune God. They understood that both prayer and ministry have to do with transformation and that transformation begins from within. And so, as lay ecclesial ministers set out to transform the world, who better to lead the way than the mystics?

MYSTICS AS MENTORS

For centuries the interior life of prayer has been compared to the state of marriage. In the *Interior Castle,* St. Teresa of Avila uses words such as betrothal, espousal and spiritual marriage to describe the deepening stages of prayer. But the language of the marriage bed did not originate with the sixteenth century Carmelite nun. The *Song of Songs* in the Old Testament, once viewed as an allegory about God and the people of Israel, is resplendent with the language of lovers. As early as the third century, Origen applied the allegory of a nuptial union to the relationship between Christ as bridegroom of the Church and to Christ, the bridegroom of the individual Christian. During the twelfth century St. Bernard of Clairvaux died while writing his eighty-sixth sermon on the *Song of Songs.* The saint has been lauded for his description of the love between Christ and the individual Christian and calls the sermons on the *Song of Songs,* "Bernard's masterpiece."[1]

While the language of lovers permeates the *Song of Songs,* similar language appears in the *Book of Hosea.* Likewise, the prophet Isaiah wrote:

> *"As a young man marries a virgin,*
> *your Builder shall marry you;*
> *And as a bridegroom rejoices in his bride*
> *so shall your God rejoice in you. "*
> *(Is 63:5).*

Scripture indicates that building the Kingdom of God is directly dependent on our relationship with the Builder who desires to bring us to the highest level of loving union.

Throughout the ages, the language of the nuptial union has offered the best description for the soul's deepest longing for God. In language that represents the deepest desire of humankind, St. Augustine declared, "You have made us for yourself, and our heart is restless until it rests in you."[2] His words suggest that the level of fulfillment that each person experiences is proportionate to the degree of their union with God. More than a metaphor, the term spiritual marriage is an experience that takes place in the depths of the soul and for this reason is known only to the one who is united to God through the consummation of that union.

Like all relationships, the journey is developmental. As persons led along this path respond to God's initiative and surrender to the ongoing graces, the journey culminates in a progressive union of wills until at last, two become one. In what might be described as a fusion of wills, persons brought to the spiritual marriage experience what John of the Cross calls a "union of likeness." Unlike the natural union by which each soul is united to God substantially, this supernatural union causes the soul to be transformed into the likeness of God.

In *The Spiritual Canticle,* John of the Cross explained "…in the union and transformation of love each gives possession of self to the other, and each leaves and exchanges self for the other."[3] In the *Ascent of Mount Carmel* he wrote:

> God's will and the soul's are in conformity, so that nothing in the one is repugnant to the other. When the soul completely rids itself of what is repugnant and unconfirmed to the divine will, it rests transformed in God through love.[4]

This supernatural "union of likeness" enables persons who are brought to the spiritual marriage to experience the fullness of their Baptismal calling. Now true children of God- those united to God through this mystical union- experience completion by becoming the person they were created to be in God. Some would argue that the term spiritual marriage is outdated. But is not this type of completion the essence of marriage when lived out in all of it is fullness through grace? Like the husband and wife who lead each other to the fullness of their unique personhood through the grace of their sacrament, so the divine Bridegroom invites each person into the bridal chamber of the heart to be transformed through grace.

Just as couples take on the values and attributes of one another as they grow more deeply in love, so persons united to God through the spiritual marriage take on the heart and the mind of God. Understandably, the effects of the supernatural union are more perfect than the union between a husband and wife for in the spiritual marriage, the Bridegroom is perfect.

While external fruits of the interior nuptials are visible in the life of persons brought to this level of intimacy, such fruits are incidental, an overflow rather than an immediate goal. This is a reality worth noting as we consider parallels within the paths of prayer and ministry.

Although the mystical marriage takes place during the final stages of the spiritual journey, and may not take place in this life, referring to it in the beginning is essential. Before we set out on a journey, we need to know the destination. Another important fact is that the invitation to a deeper relationship with God need not be concomitant with the call to active ministry. One often precedes the other but eventually, analogous stages of the two paths become apparent along the way as the two are woven together to form one stream of love.

In the *Ascent of Mount Carmel,* St. John of the Cross used the metaphor of climbing a mountain to illustrate the path toward union through prayer. Applying his metaphor to beginners in ministry provides an apt description, placing them shoulder to shoulder with beginners in prayer who stand at the foot of the mountain. Although both paths begin on separate tracks, they gradually draw closer as travelers ascend the mountain and their relationship with God deepens. And since love begets love, the fruits of the love relationship cannot be contained.

Before ministers can reach the summit of mystical union, they must develop a contemplative heart, for it is through contemplation that the soul is infused with the compassion of Christ. As the ascent continues and transformation beckons, the active apostolate and the contemplative way are no longer two distinct paths. The gradual fusion of apostolic works with the contemplative heart culminates in a union of love and a likeness of wills.

When considered in tandem, prayer and the active apostolate become the right and the left foot, advancing the pilgrim toward the apex of the mountain. Along the way, interior experiences and external events common to both paths offer insights into what John of the Cross called the active and passive nights of sense and spirit. Both paths are initiated by God and are the result of grace and involve human love, which must undergo purification.

MARRIAGE, PRAYER AND MINISTRY

In considering parallels between the stages of contemplative prayer, marriage, and lay ecclesial ministry, there are similarities worth noting. Whether a person happens to be married or celibate, male or female is not the issue. John of the Cross, Teresa of Avila and Bernard of Clairvaux were celibates, yet all found that the language of lovers best described their experience of union with God. While some suggest the language can only apply to those who are celibate, I find the language remains relevant for people in every walk of life. In fact those who are married may find it easier to relate to the language of lovers when describing their experience of union with God.

Spiritual author Father George Maloney, S.J. who has written extensively on the practice of contemplative prayer, is fond of telling married couples that they more than anyone should be able to understand the "kiss" of God. "Let him kiss me with the kisses of his mouth!" (*Song of Songs* 1:2). While the experience of spiritual union transcends the physical union, the language provides an analogy with which married couples have first-hand experience. In fact, their experience may help put to rest the criticism by some that the mystics' use of nuptial language is a sublimation that meets an unfulfilled desire for physical or sexual intimacy. On the other hand, the belief that God chooses to bring only celibates into the spiritual marriage suggests that transforming union is beyond the reach of those who are married. Both theories seem to be at odds with the teachings of mystics who have been brought to the heights of union. Teresa of Avila and John of the Cross served as spiritual directors to lay men and women, including married persons. This suggests that instructions and insights regarding the path toward union are relevant for everyone who seeks to know, love and serve God with all their heart.

Although the spiritual marriage is beyond the realm of physical intimacy, transcending feelings and emotions, it is nonetheless about the surrender of the human will to the divine; not unlike the relationship between a man and wife, as described in the in the Book of Genesis. Just as "[m]an leaves his father and mother and clings and to his wife, and the two of them become one body" (Gn 2:24b) so each person is called to leave all that keeps them from becoming one with the will of God. In the surrender of all other gods, persons become more God-like as they are transformed into the likeness of God, the very purpose for which we have been created. "And God said to them, "Be fertile and multiply; fill the earth and subdue it" (Gn.1:28). In faithful obedience to God, all are commissioned to share the fruits of that union of wills. And what is sharing those fruits if not ministry?

In *The Contemporary Challenge of St. John of the Cross,* Leonard Doohan points out that:

> [s]piritual marriage implies a mutual surrender between God and the spouse, attained by occupying one's entire being exclusively in the service of the Lord. John affirms that the quality of this loving union is more sanctifying, and of greater value to the church, than many works of service and ministry without such love.[5]

On a similar note, St. John of the Cross cautioned:

> Let those who are singularly active, who think they can win the world with their preaching and exterior works, observe here that they would profit the Church and please God more, not to mention the good example they would give, were they to spend at least half of this time with God in prayer, even though they may not have reached a prayer as sublime as this. They would certainly accomplish more and with less labor by one work than they otherwise would by a thousand.[6]

For laity who take on a more active role in church ministry, the teachings of the mystics are more important than ever as a way to integrate spiritual principles with apostolic practice. Religious communities have long recognized the need for a novitiate as a way to strengthen the novice's relationship with God before making a commitment to active ministry. While the laity cannot spend a year in a convent or monastery prior to saying "yes" to ministry, the need for them to commit to a rigorous and ongoing spiritual formation cannot be overstated.

In *Co-Workers in the Vineyard of the Lord,* published by the United States Conference of Catholic Bishops on lay ministry, the resource states, "*A living union with Christ*: For all the baptized, this union is the goal of their Christian life. For lay ecclesial ministers, it is the ground of their ministry and the irreplaceable source of its authenticity and fruitfulness."[7]

Just as prayer, when experienced at its deepest level, parallels marriage, so ministry when embraced at its deepest level parallels the prayer of union. So closely are the two intertwined that the notion that either prayer or authentic ministry could exist independent of the other is unthinkable. In discussing the seventh mansion in her *Interior Castle*, St. Teresa wrote, "this is the reason for prayer. My daughters, the purpose of this spiritual marriage: the birth always of good works, good works."[8]

That is not to say that all who embark on the path of prayer or ministry will experience the fullness of God through union in this life. Nevertheless, unless hearts and minds are directed toward this end, endless energy will be expended with little or no progress made toward union with God and perhaps only minimal effectiveness in ministry. Conversely, the more one is transformed through the love of God, the more one is able to transform the world. Thus ministry becomes the means by which God builds His Kingdom through the minister.

In the foreword to *The Practice of the Presence of God*, Henri Nouwen uses Brother Laurence, the humble doorkeeper at a Carmelite Monastery, as proof that being concerned solely with living in the presence of God does not lead the contemplative away from people but rather the contemplative is often sought out by others as a spiritual guide.[9] Nouwen used the image of the wheel to describe this phenomenon with Christ as the center of the wheel and the people of God as the spokes. The place where the spokes are closest to the center is also the place where they are closest to one another. The same holds true in the spiritual life. Drawing closer to our deepest center brings us closer to one another, a natural consequence of spiritual deepening between the bride and the Bridegroom.

As Christians, we are called to love as Christ loves. Therefore, the more our love is rooted in Christ, the more selfless our love and the more it spills over and effects the entire body. However, neither marriage, nor ministry, nor personal prayer begins on so selfless a note.

STAGES OF THE JOURNEY

The ups and downs of prayer, ministry and the married reveal parallel stages on the journey. All three begin with a period of starry-eyed courtship. When two people begin dating exclusively, their eyes may seem to be on the other person but a more honest appraisal reveals the initial attraction is motivated by selfishness. Simply put, they enjoy spending time together. The same could be said of the beginning stages of prayer and ministry. The presence of consolations during prayer and the warm glow that accompanies helping others is the most common motivator in the early stages. That is not to say it is bad; it is simply an imperfect beginning.

Healthy human beings gravitate toward people and activities they enjoy. It is only natural to want to spend time with those who make us feel good. We enjoy being around people who like us and appreciate what we do. They make us feel special and remind us that we matter. When we put this in the context of a special relationship, we call it romance. While experience or an inner skepticism may warn us that the romance stage will not last forever, we can still appreciate this stage and enjoy the feelings it generates. We may even convince ourselves that it will be permanent, that this person, or for that matter, this prayer experience or this ministry is so special that it could never be otherwise.

Depending on a number of variables and the complexities of each person's life, persons may cling to this illusion in varying degrees. The level to which they cling to the illusion will ultimately affect the level of pain they experience when the romance stage passes and, inevitably it will. This ushers in the period of disillusionment.

When speaking of marriage, the saying "the honeymoon is over" offers an apt description. In regard to prayer we allude to this period as dryness or a desert experience. In the religious life or in ministry, the phrase "first naiveté" comes to mind. Such expressions suggest the phenomenon is common. They remind us that it is the first and very necessary stage of a much larger process; others have traveled this road and we can learn from them.

Aspects of disillusionment may come and go. In the face of suffering and doubt, commitment wavers and a flood of negative emotions surface. It can be disarming at best and frightening at worst. But regardless of whether we are speaking of marriage, interior prayer, or ministry, trials and tribulations are part of the journey. Unfortunately, the tendency is to gravitate toward survival techniques and look for distractions to numb the pain. This places our spiritual health at risk, for the spiritual life demands that we set aside such diversions.

Thomas Merton addressed the importance of renouncing diversions, which he defined as "occupations and recreations provided by society that enable a man to avoid his own company for twenty-four hours a day".[10] On the same topic he wrote that no one becomes a person through diversion. "The function of diversion is simply to anesthetize the individual, as individual, and to plunge him into the warm apathetic stupor of collectivity, which like himself, wishes to remain amused."[11] Diversion masks the pain; self-reflection tears away the mask and invites both contemplatives and ministers to embrace the pain that accompanies growing more deeply in love with God.

Inner conflicts arise during each stage of life. Events and relationships, both positive and negative, trigger interior responses that affect us on a variety of levels. If unexamined, the root cause of the pleasure or inner strife will go unaddressed. Therefore, prayer and self-reflection are imperative as trials and suffering takes their toll on the human spirit. For this reason, those who embrace the spiritual path, be it through prayer or ministry, are placed in a crucible. Key to passing through this crucible is to know we are not alone and that this is a privileged time of grace. *The Book of Judith* reminds us of this very important truth.

> Besides all this, we should be grateful to the LORD our God, for putting us to the test, as he did our forefathers. Recall how he dealt with Abraham, and how he tried Isaac, and all that happened to Jacob in Syrian Mesopotamia while he was tending the flocks of Laban, his mother's brother. Not for vengeance did the Lord put them in the crucible to try their hearts, nor has he done so with us. It is by way of admonition that he chastises those who are close to him. (Jdt 8:25-27).

God continues to walk with us just as He did with the Israelites. Those who have gone before us also provide insight for the journey. How foolish we would be not to take advantage of their experience! Their wisdom serves as a road map for eventual transformation. Their God-centered approach to ministry can be likened to what John of the Cross called "the way of the perfect," which is traditionally referred to as the unitive way in the spiritual life. But whether we are speaking of prayer or ministry, degrees of perfection are reached in stages.

Following an intense period of purgation, in which heart and habits are cleansed and the mind is enlightened, persons in the unitive stage become more and more transformed in God. This stage is characterized by an attitude of holy indifference. "Not my will but Thine" is the posture of those who have reached the level of nuptial union. When hopes are dashed or things do not work out as one planned, such persons respond with acceptance rather than bitterness. Centered in God, those in the unitive stage see the world through the eyes of God and all is peace and light. This is not to say that such persons do not suffer. The lives of the saints confirm that suffering may become even more intense during this stage.

To understand better this truth we need look no further than Mary the Mother of God, whose own heart was pierced as if by a sword over and over. She remained with her Son at the foot of the cross and held His lifeless body in his arms. How great must have been her suffering and yet there was no bitterness in her. Suffering in the unitive stage is embraced as a way for the world to be purified and all is offered in union with the suffering Christ. All one's attention is focused outward in union with Christ who gave His life that the world may be one with the Father.

With the soul thus united to the heart of God, peace and pain often co-exist, but it is the peace that Jesus promised, which is not the peace of this world. Suffering is viewed by those in the unitive stage as one more offering to present to the heart of God. The soul longs for the entire world to be transformed in God and wants nothing more than to unite every effort, every sorrow, and every pain to the will of God. With motives so purified, all is regarded as efficacious in building the Kingdom of God and they see goodness everywhere.

> The strength and vehemence of love has this trait: Everything seems possible to it and it believes everyone is occupied as it is; it does not believe anyone could be employed in any other way or seek any one other than Him Whom it seeks and loves; it believes there is nothing else to occupy it and that everyone is engaged in seeking and loving Him.[12]

Persons of prayer and ministers who reach the unitive stage take on the heart and mind of Christ according to the degree that God has ordained. This is more than a mere manifestation of the virtues of Christ in the person's life. Transformed by love, these souls see others, and indeed the whole world, as a communion with Christ, who is experienced in the center of their soul. John of the Cross went so far as to say, "So great is this union that even though they differ in substance, in glory and appearance, the soul seems to be God and God seems to be the soul."[13]

A WORD OF CAUTION

As we examine ministry as a path toward union, we would do well to remember St. Teresa's advice regarding the stages of prayer. She warned against interpreting the stages of prayer in so rigid a manner that one believes passing through one stage means they will never return to it. The same could be said in regard to ministry. It is not a black and white journey. While the stages are recognizable by dominant characteristics, human nature is not that neat and tidy.

Nuances of the romance stage break into periods of disillusionment and stages of union are hardly void of trials and tribulations. The only distinction St. Teresa makes in this assessment is in regard to those who have been united through the spiritual marriage, which the saint concluded is permanent. Still, even in this state, growth continues. During the less permanent stages of union, i.e. simple union and conforming union, ongoing purification is required since God is preparing the soul for the spiritual marriage through the dark night of the spirit.

Who will be brought to the spiritual marriage is not for us to know. Recall Jesus' words, "My Father's House has many mansions." But those whose hearts remain fixed on the will of God will come to the place to which God desires to bring them. Secure in the knowledge that God is seeking them with greater longing than they are seeking God, spiritual travelers move through the crucible when human nature would prefer to avoid it. Clearly, the crucible is to ministry what the desert is to prayer. It purifies and enlightens, preparing the soul for the deepest possible union with God.

As ministers travel the path from romance, to disillusionment, to transformation, faith is the light that guides their way. According to John of the Cross, the darkness instructs the contemplative in the ways of God through the silence of unknowing. The same type of trust is required of the minister who continues to serve in the midst of uncertainty, criticism or doubt, confident that God can take the most humble offering and transform it. Just as the contemplative heart is transformed from a burning log into a living flame, so the minister who is grounded in prayer is transformed from a self-centered functionary into a God-centered offering.

It may take a lifetime and the spiritual traveler may not reach full communion with God in this life, but understanding the process serves as a reminder that authentic ministry must be rooted in God. Ministers may be confirmed by community, but it is God who calls and anoints them, leading them ever deeper into the heart of God. As the partnership between humanity and divinity grows deeper and more permanent, two wills become one. In wordless surrender, the lives of those who are brought to this level of union, echo the words of the dying Savior who raised his eyes to heaven, and cried out in a loud voice, "Father, into your hands I commend my spirit" (Lk 23:46).

Please complete the exercises on the following page before reading chapter two.

TIMELINE

Using the timeline below, chart your relationship with God. The plus lines represent movement toward a deeper awareness of God in your life. The minus lines represent times when you felt distanced from God. Place a circle around times when you experienced moments of conversion.

+5____

+4____

+3____

+2____

+1____

Years in age:

5 10 13 17 21 25 30 35 40 45 50 60 70

-1____

-2____

-3____

-4____

-5____

* The ages on the chart represent critical stages in human development and affect the spiritual journey.

Name the people who were teachers, mentors and those who provided inspiration along the way, bringing you to where you are today on your spiritual journey. Do not forget the saints, authors and those you have never met but have had an impact on your life.

Childhood:____

Adolescence:____

Youngadulthood:____

Thirties:____

Forties:____

Fifties:____

Sixties:____

Seventies:____

CHAPTER II
ROMANCE

HUMAN DYNAMICS OF A DIVINE CALL

Thomas Merton wrote: "Man cannot live without love and if the love is not genuine then he must have a substitute – a corruption of real love."[1]

Merton goes on to explain that false forms of love sacrifice the real for the conceptual and exist only in the mind. One such form of love, according to Merton, is romance. "Romantic love sacrifices the persons and values that are present and actual, to other values that are always out of reach."[2] His analysis may explain why romance is short lived and represents an ideal which often contradicts reality. The phenomenon of falling in love with love seems to validate Merton's view and is personified by young girls who dream of Prince Charming and teenage boys who fantasize about the girl who is a perfect ten. While such behavior may be amusing in children and adolescents, when carried into adulthood, it can be the source of a painful awakening.

Since romance is a mental construct, a product of the imagination, it fails to reflect real life. Nevertheless, more often than not, it is the way relationships or projects begin. People are on their best behavior during the beginning stage of a relationship. A new career or project gives rise to emotions aptly described by the saying, "the world is my oyster." Feelings of invincibility are fed by the adrenaline rush present when a dream or aspiration beckons. For the inexperienced minister, it can translate into unrealistic expectations and the belief that every seed planted will bear fruit.

But lest we become too critical of this emotionally-driven, but necessary stage, we do well to ponder the description that John of the Cross set forth in regard to prayer as experienced by beginners. In *The Dark Night*, the sixteenth century mystic points out that even God takes advantage of what more experienced pilgrims might consider human weakness. The saint wrote:

> It should be known then that God nurtures and caresses the soul, after it has been resolutely converted to his service, like a loving mother who warms her child with the heat of her bosom, nurses it with good milk and tender food, and carries and caresses it in her arms.[3]

He portrays God as a mother who woos the inexperienced person along the path of prayer through consolations that are both sense oriented and spiritually satisfying. Basking in the delight that accompanies this stage, the novice finds the encouragement needed to continue the search for God. Regardless of whether that search is initiated along the path of prayer or the path of ministry, the period of romance plays an important role.

Romance is characterized by people or events that entice and captivate our interest. It appeals to us on a sensory or emotional level and lessons learned seem to be realized only after spiritual seekers move beyond it. Distance affords the type of clarity that comes with hindsight and logic seems to supply the reason for this phenomenon.

If the faults of the other person were blatantly apparent from the very beginning, red flags would prematurely squelch any desire to pursue intimate relationships. Few people would embark on the path of deepening prayer if the dark night of sense or spirit was their first experience of prayer. And, would anyone say, "Yes" to ministry if they had not first felt loved for their uniqueness as a child of God or as a valued member of a community? The truth is, most of us fall in love with the ideal before we are able to commit to the real.

When Jesus first called Simon Peter, Andrew, James and John, he promised them something that was more exciting than catching fish. "Come after me and I will make you fishers of men." (Mt 4:19) The invitation was so intriguing that Scripture tells us they immediately abandoned their nets and followed him.

Luke's Gospel paints an even more exciting picture. He wrote that when Jesus came upon Peter and Andrew while cleaning their nets after a fruitless night of fishing, He got into the boat and from there continued teaching the crowds. When He finished, He told Simon Peter, "[p]ut out into deep water and lower your nets for a catch." (Lk 5:4) to which Simon Peter responded, "Master we have worked hard all night and have caught nothing, but at your command I will lower the nets for a catch." (Lk 5:5) When they had done this they caught so many fish that their nets were beginning to break (Lk 5:7). Overwhelmed, Simon Peter cried out, "Depart from me Lord, for I am a sinful man!" (Lk 5:8) But Jesus responded by extending both an invitation and a promise. "Do not be afraid; from now on you will be catching men." (Lk 5:10)

Time and again Scripture illustrates that Jesus met people where they were. If it took a miracle, Jesus provided a miracle. Peter, and later his mother-in-law who was healed by Jesus, were moved to action by wonder and gratitude. But such illustrations are not limited to Biblical times.

AFFIRMED BY COMMUNITY

Carrie and Steve experienced a tremendous healing during a Marriage Encounter Weekend. They felt God's love in a way that was unlike anything they had known and were overwhelmed with gratitude. After the weekend, Carrie and Steve were invited to attend a Team Training Weekend with the possibility of becoming a presenting couple on future weekends. The invitation was like icing on the cake. They were closer than they had been in years and saying "Yes" to the team seemed a perfect way to thank God. It was also a way to keep alive the gift which they had received during the weekend. When they were selected to be a team couple, they felt affirmed and blessed. Like the apostles, Carrie and Steve had no idea where saying "Yes" would lead them. They had no idea of the sacrifices their ministry would involve. They only knew they had been touched by God and in the process felt they had been anointed.

Just as the apostles discovered the cost of discipleship over time, so Carrie and Steve learned that being a team couple entailed sacrifices. It meant they would have to commit to writing talks, assume a leadership role within the local Marriage Encounter community and be away from their children whenever they were part of a weekend. On the plus side, they would be part of a group of people they saw as role models. In a sense they were part of the inner circle. It was not exclusive, but it was special. They had been called and they would never quite be the same. Like the apostles, discipleship beckoned, engaging their hearts and their imaginations. Reality would come later.

• • •

Dan felt restless. Some might call it a mid-life crisis. He had achieved all his goals by age forty-five. He had gone about as far as he cared to go professionally, was happily married, had a beautiful home and his children were doing well. And yet, he felt as if something was missing. Life seemed stale. One evening he attended a RCIA meeting for sponsors. The bulletin announcement invited people to "Come and see." There was no commitment involved in attending the first meeting so he figured he had nothing to lose. But as Dan listened to the RCIA director share her experience of working with candidates and catechumens for over fifteen years, Dan was moved. He saw something in her that he wanted. He envied her obvious love for God and the Church. Hoping to catch what she had, Dan agreed to be a sponsor. The experience proved to be a positive one. As he accompanied Jack, his catechumen, toward the Sacraments of Initiation, Dan's faith was strengthened.

He began to re-examine the faith he had taken for granted. Each week Dan came away with a deeper yearning for more. Religion used to be a duty; now it was exciting. As he continued his search, he prayed and read Scripture daily. He felt at peace and in the process he began falling in love with God. Two years later Dan enrolled in the diocesan graduate program and earned a master's degree in religious education. Eventually he quit his job and was hired as the Minister of Christian Formation at St. Edward's parish. Life was good and Dan felt privileged to be embarking on a new career at this stage of his life.

ꟷ • • • ꟷ

In the world of advertising it is called "a hook." As a way to invite others into the faith journey we say, "Come and see." The approach piques one's curiosity and appeals to a basic hunger for more than what we currently have. When Andrew asked Jesus where he lived, Jesus responded by saying, "Come and See." The implication was that discipleship was a process that could only be learned through experience and that experience meant walking with Jesus. Over time, the risks would be revealed but by then, hopefully, faith and trust would overcome challenges that are also part of discipleship.

ꟷ • • • ꟷ

When many of her friends were losing interest in religion, Jackie's interest in God seemed to peak. She had attended a retreat in high school which proved to be one of the high points of her junior year. During her senior year, Jackie joined the parish youth group and on a missionary trip to Appalachia, felt drawn to work in the area of social justice. While in college, Jackie was active in campus ministry, but after she got married, her life became very busy. It was not until she enrolled her daughter in the parish religious education program that Jackie thought about helping out at the parish. The high school confirmation class was looking for adult mentors and since the meetings were held the same time as her daughter's class, she decided to volunteer. In no time Jackie felt she had found her niche.

She connected with the youth in a way that surprised even her. After helping for several months, the pastor asked Jackie if she would consider being the parish Youth Minister. It would be a volunteer position for the remainder of the year but hopefully, by next year it would become a salaried position. The money did not really matter to Jackie. She enjoyed being with the young people. Her love for peace and justice issues had been rekindled and the youth's response to the projects she initiated was more than she had expected. Jackie was thrilled. Inwardly, she was flattered that the pastor thought she was up to the job of being a youth minister and she felt energized by the affirmation. The feeling she had experienced in college - that God was her best friend - was back and her life seemed to have a new purpose.

The four ministers cited above share one thing in common. Carrie, Steve, Dan, and Jackie were all on a high. Feelings such as gratitude, fulfillment, affirmation and appreciation were not only present but were largely the driving force behind their saying "Yes" to ministry. They had fallen in love with an ideal, which is the way most of us begin the journey. But how we fare in the long run has a lot to do with the way we adjust once the rose colored glasses come off.

When ministry begins on a high, there is only one way to go and that is down. It may come as a rude awakening, but it is bound to happen. Nevertheless, ministry is about more than feelings or few would persevere. Like conversion, being called to ministry is not a once and done event. It happens over and over within the context of current challenges and involves the daily decision to remain faithful. As new ministers meet reality head on, support and guidance from those who are more experienced can help the new minister understand that ministry entails moving from the high that comes with a flood of warm feelings to the pain that comes with being lifted high on the cross. Until ministers experience both, they have not really experienced ministry.

When we respond only to what feels good, we are, in fact, serving ourselves. But like a child at its mother's breast, those new to ministry are gradually weaned. God nudges them gently into a world they could not have anticipated when their hearts leapt with joy at the thought of walking with the Master.

IMPORTANCE OF SELF-KNOWLEDGE

Although the apostles walked with Jesus and observed His miracles first hand, they regularly misinterpreted the signs. They quarreled among themselves, vied for places of honor and succumbed to jealousy. They were often scared and in times of danger they struggled with doubt. When Jesus was arrested, they ran away. They clung to the idea of an earthly Kingdom even after the Resurrection because they heard what they wanted to hear. They lived out of their imagination and expected Jesus to conform to their notion of the Kingdom of God.

And yet, those early years, including the mistakes and misconceptions, were important enough to be included in the Gospels. Their human failings teach us a great deal about serving God and one another. They teach us there is more to discipleship than what we first imagine, that every step of the journey counts and that God continues to form us through life experiences and the guidance of the Holy Spirit.

Spiritual writer Leonard Doohan addressed the importance of building on past experience by recalling the words of John of the Cross during his search for deeper union with God. Doohan wrote, "By the age of 25, John has learned that ministry, education, religious life and theology do not automatically insure union with God."[4] He goes on to say, "[w]hat he has he values but, without despising previous experiences, he leaves them aside to continue the search of new ways."[5]

Experiences, both good and bad, provide valuable insights into human behavior. They reveal things about us that we could not have known otherwise. More often than not, unconscious motivations are discovered only when relationships go awry and conflicts disclose hidden agendas. When hubris manifests itself as a need for recognition or control, relationships become secondary and may trigger responses that take us by surprise. As painful as self-knowledge can be, no one advances in the spiritual life without it. Without self-knowledge, ministers run the risk of performing good works for the wrong reasons.

Socrates said, "The unexamined life is not worth living." His theory suggests that every event and the interior response that follows invite the self-reflective person to incorporate lessons from the past with present challenges. Both positive and negative experiences can lead to spiritual deepening for those who are open to learn. Therefore, nothing about life should be trivialized or discounted, for as Scripture reminds us, "[a] ll things work for good for those who love God" (Rom 8:28).

Teresa of Avila stressed the absolute necessity of self-knowledge during the beginning stages of the spiritual life. In her description of the soul as a castle with seven dwelling places and thousands of rooms in each, she wrote about the room of self-knowledge in her treatment of the second dwelling place.

> Let it [the soul] walk through these dwelling places which are up above, down below and to the sides, since God has given it such great dignity. Don't force it to stay too long in one room alone. Oh, but if it is the room of self-knowledge! How necessary this room is – see that you understand me...Here it will discover its lowliness.[6]

Discovering our lowliness is not about self-deprecation. In *Thoughts in Solitude,* Thomas Merton called the practice of turning away in disgust from personal fault, illusions, and mistakes a form of self annihilation.[7] He pointed out that to know and experience our own nothingness, we must also love it. And we can only love it when we see what is good in it. This happens over time and with the help of grace. It is what is known as humility and humility is about discovering our lowliness and understanding that everything good in us has its origin in God. It was humility that allowed St. Paul to exclaim, "I will rather boast most gladly of my weakness, in order that the power of Christ may dwell with me." (2 Cor 12:9) But Paul did not come to this realization without a struggle. Indeed, he confessed,

> Therefore, that I might not become too elated, a thorn in the flesh was given to me, an angel of Satan, to beat me, to keep me from being too elated. Three times I begged the Lord about this, that it might leave me, but he said to me 'My grace is sufficient for you, for power is made perfect in weakness.' (2 Cor 12:7-9).

As the illusion of romance fades, God continues to beckon but in ways that are unfamiliar. For those who dare to proceed, a new understanding awaits. In the absence of sensory satisfaction, the soul's gaze is turned inward where it will encounter both its own misery and the wonder and grandeur of God. As disillusionment sets in, God instructs the soul in secret. But this divine instruction is only the beginning for those who persevere in what will become a life long journey of intermittent periods of darkness and light.

Once the journey has begun, persons of prayer are called to relinquish their fondness for consolations. At this stage, ministers are called to relinquish their dependence on affirmation and look beyond approval as a bench mark for success. As ministers become more spiritually mature, they will learn there is another standard by which to measure the fruits of the spiritual life. Like those who travel the path of prayer, ministers will be invited to direct their focus away from self toward God who is inviting them into a deeper relationship. But before this can happen, they must experience the heartache of disillusionment.

Before transitioning from the romance stage to a more realistic understanding, take a few moments to reflect on your call to ministry. At the end of each chapter journaling questions have been provided to help guide your reflections. This is a journey in self discovery; so there is no need to rush. Recall that God is inviting you into a deeper understanding of His love and His plan for you.

JOURNALING QUESTIONS

1. When and where did you first experience the call to ministry?
2. What attracted you?
3. What were your fears or concerns?
4. How did you respond?
5. What expectations did you bring to the ministry?
6. Have those expectations changed?
7. How do you view your first attractions and expectations in light of your experience now?

CHAPTER III
DISILLUSIONMENT

FROM ROMANCE TO REALITY

Bernard of Clairvaux lamented that many in the Church were quick to offer others what they had only begun to experience themselves. It prompted the twelfth century mystic to write:

> So urgent is the charity of those through whom the streams of heavenly doctrine flow that they want to pour it forth before they have been filled. They are more ready to speak than to listen, impatient to teach what they have not grasped, and full of presumption to govern others while they know not how to govern themselves.[1]

The saint's observation seems to take aim at those who are captivated by the first fervors of the active apostolate. Though undeniably harsh, his assessment of the romantic stage is valid and as true today as when it was written. It also strongly resembles John of the Cross's description of those who are new to prayer. Assessing beginners with the same type of candor the Carmelite friar wrote

> [t]he soul finds its joy therefore in spending lengthy periods at prayer, perhaps even entire nights; its penances are pleasures; its fasts, happiness; and the sacraments and spiritual conversations are its consolations. Although spiritual persons do practice these exercises with great profit and persistence and are very careful about them, spiritually speaking, they conduct themselves in a very weak and imperfect manner... and since these persons have not had time to acquire those firm habits, their work must of necessity be feeble, like that of little children.[2]

Those who are motivated simply by the joy and satisfaction they receive from working in ministry are like those who cling to consolations received during prayer. Filled with enthusiasm and good intentions, they leave the starting line sprinting but often fail to go the distance. Most new ministers lack the wisdom that comes with time and experience and even failure. Unknowingly, they rely on positive reinforcement to sustain them, mistaking it for grace. Carried away by feelings of excitement, they devote an inordinate amount of time to work in an effort to win the approval of others, often sacrificing prayer time or neglecting personal responsibilities.

They tend to measure success by numbers and are easily offended by opposing views. They may dismiss negative criticisms as irrelevant or become completely demoralized by them. They believe they are serving God when in truth they are merely satisfying their own desires. Seeking and basking in immediate gratification places them at risk. When all goes well, they believe they are doing the will of God; but when reality falls short of their expectations, they begin to question their call to ministry. And so they enter the stage of disillusionment.

Disillusionment takes ministers from romance to reality and is crucial if ministers are to embrace their calling in a selfless manner. The stage of disillusionment prepares novices for the sacrificial dimension of the active apostolate as the imaginary view of ministry gives way to a more realistic understanding. And, nothing brings this reality home as clearly as an encounter with human frailty.

As one church minister put it, "the view from inside is very different than the view from the outside."

This is not an indictment against the Church, but simply a recognition that romance tends to glorify reality. As romantic notions of ministry dissipate, ministers are invited to recommit to ministry as it is being lived out day-by-day.

Coming face-to-face with human frailty, those new to ministry can easily become discouraged. Without the spiritual undergirding, ministers depend more on their own capabilities than on God's grace. Some deal with such crises by redoubling their efforts, thus becoming as weary as they are frustrated. Others go through the motions or leave ministry all together. Fight or flight reactions may numb the pain, but they do little to deepen self-awareness.

Like persons of prayer, ministers soon learn that those who link their hearts to the delight of the senses are actually setting themselves up for bitterness and suffering. As John of the Cross explained, "[t]he extent of the torment, blindness and weakness will correspond to the weakening of grace brought on by the appetites."[3] Some may consider John's choice of the word torment a bit too strong. But like any addiction, the more a person relies on a temporary "fix" to maintain a state of well-being, the greater the suffering will be in the absence of that "fix."

When it comes to the interior life, ministers must learn to rely less on outcomes validated by tangible results than on their love for God, since intentionality is a more reliable indicator of spiritual efficacy. Both positive and negative experiences have the potential to take ministers to the realm of everlasting truth but only to the degree with which they move beyond the realm of self. When discouragement threatens to overtake them, these ministers would do well to heed the words of the Carmelite saint who wrote, "All the world's wisdom and human ability contrasted with the wisdom of God is pure and utter ignorance."[4]

Those who seek the wisdom of God through self-emptying are guided by the

Holy Spirit. Over time, seekers discover that people and life situations continually change. Approval may be strong one day and non-existent the next. And so, previous imaginary ideas of ministry begin to crumble in light of real life experiences.

Much like coming to the realization that the right toothpaste will not guarantee finding the love of your life, ministers come to realize that working in and for the Church is not a fast track to holiness. As romance fades, disillusionment calls ministers to put aside an earlier naiveté. Each person encounters disillusionment in a slightly different manner, yet the lessons to be learned are universal, regardless of the form disillusionment takes.

FACES OF DISILLUSIONMENT

Joan, an extraordinary minister of the Eucharist at St. Patrick's Church, had been taking communion to the sick and the homebound for several months. As a retired health care worker who spent most of her life working with the sick, it seemed like the perfect ministry and Joan felt blessed to be able to serve her parish in this way. Wednesdays quickly became the highlight of her week. She regarded the Scripture lessons which she shared with those she visited as her gift to the suffering Body of Christ.

But as Joan got to know the people she visited, the feeling that she was ministering to them was replaced by a sense of unworthiness. Her life seemed so easy compared to theirs that it made her feel uneasy. The people she visited had such faith and accepted their suffering in a way that led Joan to believe it was they who should be ministering to her. Conflicted by self-doubt and feelings of unworthiness, Joan began to question her call to ministry.

• • •

As a team couple, Steve and Carrie felt distraught when three couples left early during their first Marriage Encounter weekend as team. When one of the couples left immediately following one of their talks, Carrie was convinced it was something she had said that turned the couple off. Her imagining that she was responsible for the couple's leaving early burst the balloon that had been inflated by a false sense of her own importance as a member of the team.

• • •

In a similar manner, Jackie's bubble was burst when her appointment as parish youth minister was announced. Two volunteers with whom she had worked side by side and whom she had regarded as friends now became distant and unavailable when she approached them to help with activities. Later Jackie learned they were making disparaging remarks about her leadership skills behind her back. Jackie was devastated. Conflicted by self-doubt, Jackie wondered if she had made a mistake in accepting the position of parish Youth Minister.

ꟷ • • • ꟷ

Ministers often feel humbled as they stand in the light of others. Or they may feel betrayed by criticism, rejection or the apathy of others toward a particular project. As doubts and questions begin to surface, those new to ministry may find themselves wondering, "What do I possibly have to offer?" "Who am I that I should call anyone to a life of holiness?" Or, "What am I doing wrong?" While self-doubt can catch the neophyte off guard, it is a valuable part of the growth process. Those in the throws of self doubt do well to reflect on the words of St. Therese of Lisieux who reminded her sisters in Carmel that God does not call those who are worthy, but those whom He pleases. Her reminder is one that ministers may find helpful when bombarded with feelings of inadequacy or unworthiness. Similarly, Mother Teresa of Calcutta warned her sisters that when moods fluctuate, the root cause is often pride. Both admonitions help ministers examine motives that may be buried within their desire to serve.

Acknowledging personal limitations helps rid ministers of self-righteous thinking or the need to judge themselves or others. As old ways of thinking begin to crumble, conflicted souls become more open to the wisdom of others. They begin to place their trust in God as they search for a deeper understanding of their calling. This proved true for Joan.

• • •

As Joan prayed and reflected about her feelings of unworthiness, she realized that her discomfort was actually rooted in an unconscious sense of superiority. As a result, she was surprised by the faith of the people she visited. The reality conflicted with the notion that she was the one doing the giving. Prior to her getting to know these graced souls, Joan assumed the minister was the only one who had something to give.

The experience was humbling, but it taught Joan about the reciprocal dimension of ministry. Over time she understood that she had been called to minister to the sick, not because she was more faith-filled or a better person, but because she was in a position to do so and because she was willing. Once Joan stopped measuring her faith against the faith of others, she was able to focus on the people she visited and trust that God could use her however he chose. This new insight allowed Joan to celebrate the faith of the shut-ins whom she visited without questioning her own calling.

• • •

For Jackie, who wrongly assumed that everyone would share her excitement about her appointment as youth minister, the sting of rejection and criticism was devastating. In reflecting on her inclination to resign her position, she realized that she was simply trying to escape the pain of rejection and that saying "Yes" to ministry meant moving beyond personal disappointment. Jackie realized that she could not reach out to the larger community through works of justice and peace while harboring feelings of resentment toward those who had hurt her. Love was a decision just as surely as her commitment to serve was a decision. Eventually, prayer and grace gave Jackie the courage to reach out to those who were judging her, but it was not easy.

• • •

In a similar manner, Carrie realized she was not in control of other people's behavior. She had to learn to meet each couple where they were, to do her part and then leave the rest to God. In shifting the focus from herself to the couples, Carrie became more compassionate. Over time disappointment and self-doubt were replaced by a deeper appreciation for the uniqueness of every couple's relationship. The experience also helped Carrie come to terms with her role as a presenter. It helped her understand that she was simply a facilitator and that the dynamics of the weekend were about more than presentations by the team. In letting go of the importance she had placed on her role, she was able to be more open to the presence of the Holy Spirit and felt less anxious about her own limitations. She understood that it was God who changes hearts, and how and when that happens may not have been for her to know. This new awareness allowed her to view her ministry as a way to plant seeds and to trust in God's grace in a way that had previously eluded her.

• • •

Each minister experienced disillusionment in a different manner, yet each learned something about their call to serve that had eluded them while they were in the romance stage. Seemingly negative experiences led to greater self knowledge and an increase in humility. As a result, they were able to move beyond the realm of purely natural inclinations.

A CALL TO HUMILITY

Those who are new to prayer or ministry are tempted to imagine they are further along the spiritual path than is the case. As a result, warnings to walk humbly often go unheeded since the beginner's understanding of the virtue of humility is flawed. But humility is essential if progress is to be made in the ascent toward union by both persons of prayer and ministers.

St. Bernard called humility the first rung on the ladder of the spiritual life. In the epilogue of *The Interior Castle* Teresa of Avila wrote, "He [the Lord] is very fond of humility. By considering that you do not merit to enter even the third [mansion], you will quickly win favor to reach the fifth."[5] In the same work she stressed that humility is foundational and that unless humility is present, the Lord will not construct a high building since it will eventually fall to the ground.

In *The Dark Night*, John of the Cross expounded on the importance of humility by first shedding light on the dangers of pride in the beginning stages of prayer.

> These beginners feel so fervent and diligent in their spiritual exercises and undertakings that a certain kind of secret pride is generated in them which begets a complacency with themselves and their accomplishments, despite the fact that holy works do of their very nature cause humility.[6]

Those who travel the spiritual path, be it through prayer or ministry, will quickly encounter interior and external obstacles. Though unpleasant, such experiences nurture the virtue of humility, allowing it to take root and grow. Confronted by human frailty, Joan, Jackie, Carrie, and Steve decided to reject illusions based on an earlier naiveté. Through prayerful reflection, personal shortcomings were revealed. Grace provided the strength to continue the journey and to walk more humbly with God, despite obstacles encountered along the way.

Ministers whose work places them in a highly visible role can also be at risk. Mother Teresa of Calcutta counseled her sisters about this when she wrote:

> [o]ur life being so much in the public eye, has the more need for humility. We go about doing good to the people and so they surround us with love and respect and trust. This is why we need humility – to protect us in danger, to guard us from falls, to guarantee the fruitfulness of our works of charity.[7]

But sometimes pride manifests when ministers feel underappreciated. They may resent the attention that religious or clergy receive, while their efforts often go unrecognized. Yet hurtful situations can become a source of spiritual growth if ministers spend time reflecting on Jesus who emptied Himself and became a servant to all. The Son of God was often misunderstood, rejected and in the end was betrayed by one of his own. When ministers keep their eyes on Jesus, they are less apt to stumble and fall as a result of feelings that indulge in self-pity.

NOT-SO-SWEET SUCCESS

Wherever God is at work, so is temptation. When early expectations crumble, the temptation to abandon prayer and/or ministry is also present. But temptation is not always precipitated by a negative experience. Sometimes too much success can catch up with new ministers as was the case for Dan.

• • •

Dan seemed to transition into his new position as Minister of Religious Education at St. Edwards with little difficulty. He was pleasantly surprised by the reception he received from the people of the parish. As a skilled public speaker, he was at ease in front of groups and people often complimented him, not only about his presentation skills, but also about the content. Word got around and Dan's adult formation programs quickly became very popular. People from neighboring parishes often attended his conferences and as the numbers grew, so did Dan's ego.

Although he was careful to give credit to the Holy Spirit whenever he was praised, Dan found that inwardly he was becoming critical of those who were not as gifted. He found it increasingly difficult to listen to the pastor's homilies and found that he was making judgments about the priest. Eventually Dan's criticism of the pastor affected how he interacted with him.

• • •

Prosperity, satisfaction or consolation can make beginners smug, which is another example of how pride becomes an obstacle for ministers. Becoming overly confident or preoccupied with how we are perceived by others are direct contradictions to the virtue of humility. This truth was underscored by St. Teresa who wrote, "[f]or humility implies detachment from one's self, from worry about esteem or honor."[8]

Recall that Jesus praised the publican in the back of the temple, who not daring to raise his eyes to heaven, beat his breast and prayed, "O God, be merciful to me a sinner" (Lk 18:13). And that Jesus contrasted the demeanor of publican with the Pharisee who boasted of all he had done, thanking God that he was not like other men.

Few ministers would engage in such obvious self-aggrandizement. But pride subtly makes its way into human hearts and ministers are hardly immune. Addiction to praise, an insatiable need for approval or a messiah complex are all symptoms of a greater problem. Ministry can become a way to meet a minister's unhealthy ego needs, which is another reason why self-knowledge is imperative.

• • •

When the numbers fell, Dan had to come to terms with the manner in which personal satisfaction had been driving his efforts. He realized that pride had turned his gift into an obstacle to his relationship with God. How could he profess to love the God he could not see when he was being less than kind to the people God had also chosen to do his work? By comparing the pastor's speaking skills to his own, Dan failed to recognize that God works through people in ways he could not appreciate when he was blinded by pride and self-love.

He came to this understanding through an unlikely source. While leafing through a magazine, Dan came across an article written by Fred Rogers of Public Television's famed *Mr. Roger's Neighborhood.* While in the seminary, Mr. Rogers who was an ordained Presbyterian minister and frequently visited churches to observe the preaching style of clergy. On one such occasion, he turned to a friend after listening to the sermon and was about to comment on the poor quality of it when he noticed tears in his friend's eyes. The friend looked at him and said, "That man said exactly what I needed to hear."

Mr. Roger's story helped Dan place his role as presenter in perspective. It invited him to see the pastor through a different set of lenses once he realized that ministry was about more than being a gifted speaker. The experience reminded Dan that it is the Spirit of God working in the heart of the listeners that transforms hearts and that God uses both the gifted and the seemingly not-so-gifted to bring about his Kingdom. The experience provided a valuable lesson for Dan. Not only did it help him to be more humble, but it made him realize how he had fallen prey to self-deception. As a result, Dan decided to seek the counsel of a spiritual director on a regular basis.

SPIRITUAL GUIDANCE

Both John and Teresa wrote about the importance of spiritual guidance for those pursuing the path to union. A spiritual director plays an important role in the spiritual development for all who take their relationship with God seriously. But, unless a spiritual guide leads the directee along the path of humility and detachment, the spiritual director can easily function like a blind person leading the blind. About such directors, John of the Cross warned, "They do not guide them [directees] along the paths of humility but give them a free hand in this matter, which causes them a want of the true spirit of faith."[9]

Although the saint is referring to consolations and extraordinary experiences during prayer, a parallel can be drawn with those in ministry. Pride and a desire for affirmation are common obstacles to spiritual growth. When a spiritual director allows the minister's focus to remain fixed on seeming successes or failures without assessing the possibility of pride or attachment, an opportunity to grow in self-knowledge is lost. This explains why Teresa insisted that spiritual guides should be both learned and experienced in the ways of God.

• • •

Teresa's wisdom reminds me of an incident shared by a seasoned pastoral associate. She recalled that as a new minister, she walked into her spiritual director's office and reported feeling overwhelmed and physically exhausted by the demands of her role in the parish. The wise director reminded her that Jesus already saved the world, and so there was no reason for her to do it again. "Your role is to plant seeds. You are just one small part of the process. Why not do what you can and leave the rest to God?" The gentle reminder by her spiritual director helped her focus on *why* she thought she had to do everything herself. The director guided her toward addressing underlying psychological needs that had led to unhealthy behavior patterns.

• • •

Linda had been a straight-A student, but not without a lot of hard work. Her efforts were reinforced by her parents' praise, which she equated with their love. With the help of her director, she realized that she had transferred the behavior pattern to her relationship with God. She worked tirelessly to win God's approval, which she equated with praise and affirmation from others. By suggesting that Linda spend time meditating on God's unconditional love she was able to approach her work in a more realistic manner.

ꟹ • • • ꟹ

Working through situations which John would regard as the night of sense ultimately brings inner peace. As John pointed out, "Many blessings flow from the harmony and tranquility of the four natural passions – joy, hope, fear and sorrow."[10] When there is discord, exploring the reason behind the lack of harmony provides valuable insights.

Words we may not want to hear or circumstances we would prefer not to deal with often trigger insights that help us grow. A wise spiritual guide will frame questions in a way that will challenge even as they support and encourage the person seeking guidance. Each experience, when handled wisely, can serve to fortify the soul for the next test of faith.

From a practical perspective, the choice of a spiritual director should not be undertaken without prayer and research. It is important to choose someone who has been trained as a spiritual guide and whom you respect as a person of prayer with knowledge of the spiritual path. Unlike a life coach or a therapist, whose goal is to solve problems, the goal of the spiritual director is to guide those entrusted to their care toward deeper intimacy with God. Though not essential, it is helpful if a spiritual director has a background in psychology or some experience with the science of human behavior. This allows for a more integrative approach regarding the interplay between mind, body and spirit.

Interviewing a potential spiritual director regarding education, experience and their particular approach to spiritual direction should precede any commitment to the relationship. It is important to discuss why the person is seeking direction at this time and what, if any, expectations they bring to the relationship. It may help to formalize the relationship with an understanding that it can be terminated if either party finds the relationship is no longer helpful to the directee.

Regularly scheduled meetings, usually on a monthly basis, can provide encouragement and insight and can foster a more disciplined approach to the spiritual life. Through a process of careful listening and questioning, the spiritual director can help the directee discover how God is calling the person into a deeper relationship. This holds true for those on the path of prayer as well as ministry. If one is serious about the spiritual life, spiritual direction should be ongoing and not sought merely during times of crises. Still, every wise director understands that the real spiritual guide is the Holy Spirit and that a human guide is merely a facilitator, helping the directee to recognize the action of the Holy Spirit along the way.

That having been said, there may be times when an actual spiritual guide is not available. Then, spiritual books or a trusted friend who has reached a level of spiritual maturity can provide guidance in a less formal manner. In the absence of a formal spiritual guide, the Holy Spirit continues to guide those who are open and seek ways to deepen their relationship with God. In my own life I have found that when I wanted a spiritual director, one was not always available, but during those times when I truly needed one, God provided and the right person seemed to come along.

STANDING AT THE CROSSROADS

Having traveled the path of romance and disillusionment, ministers stand at the first of many forks in the road that leads to union. Gone is an earlier naiveté and in its place is a more realistic view of what discipleship entails. At this stage, some will turn away, but those who humbly embrace their calling will follow the path that beckons and continue their commitment to build the Kingdom of God through participation in ecclesial ministry as co-workers in the vineyard. Almost in spite of themselves, these individuals seem to trust the unknown because to turn away would be unthinkable. Their hearts seem to echo the words of St. Peter when the Lord asked the disciples if they too would desert Him. And Simon Peter responded, "Master, to whom shall we go? You have the words of eternal life" (Jn 6:68).

As a retreat facilitator and a spiritual director, I have found this is the stage where most ministers begin seeking guidance and support. Although they are confident about their call to ministry, they realize how difficult the path before them can be. Through encounters with more experienced ministers, they have observed that some seem to go through the motions, while others are genuinely joy-filled. Afraid that ministry will become like any other job, wise co-workers in the Lord's vineyard look for ways to prevent this from happening. This typically takes place during the first five years, but it could be sooner or later, depending on the individual's experience, personal strengths and expectations.

❧ • • • ❧

One parish minister told me that she thought everyone in ministry eventually burned out. She was surrounded by people who seemed to be operating in that mode and she fell into the same pattern of thinking. Although she was committed, her lack of joy was apparent. As her spiritual guide, my challenge was to help her understand that burnout is not synonymous with longevity and then guide her along the path of joyful surrender.

❧ • • • ❧

A similar experience involved a pastor of a large and very busy parish who contacted me to facilitate a retreat for the staff which was overworked and exhibiting signs of stress. He was quick to point out that they needed more than directives regarding a healthy diet, adequate rest, supportive friendships and leaving work behind when they left for the day. He understood that holy ministers need more than a balanced life and quick fixes. While the appraisal of personal habits is a good starting place, the spiritual life requires more than a change in behavior patterns.

• • •

Changing personal habits may treat the symptoms, but will do little to address the cause. Pop psychology and the self-help approach focus on feeling better; inner healing is rooted in the desire to do God's will. One focuses on changing behavior patterns; the other leads to greater self-knowledge. It is the difference between self-indulgence and spiritual healing.

Spiritual healing takes place in the inner depths of the soul and is facilitated by the process of self-emptying. Healing requires self-knowledge and mastery over the senses and can only be accomplished with God's grace. It requires letting go in order to let God work in our lives as God sees fit. This happens in stages and may take a lifetime. For despite the best of intentions, Baptismal garments become soiled, resolutions dissipate and natural instincts gravitate toward the pleasure principle. Yet surrendering to the grace of the moment makes each step along the way sacred. It invites travelers to respond to a higher calling. The practice of putting God first is the only way to begin the process of self-emptying, but few can travel this path without human support as well as divine. In *The Science of the Cross,* St. Edith Stein explained that God created us and desires us for himself. But as the saint pointed out,

> ...the way is narrow, steep and difficult. Most people remain en route. A few manage to get beyond the first beginnings – a dwindling small number arrive at the goal. That is due to dangers on the way – worldly dangers, the evil enemy, and one's own nature – but also due to ignorance and lack of qualified guidance. Souls do not understand what is happening within them, and seldom is someone to be found who could open their eyes to what is going on. To these John offers a competent guide.[11]

As the sacred unknown beckons, the ways of God become increasingly unfamiliar, yet obstacles encountered along the way awaken persons of prayer and those in ministry to the importance of traveling by the narrow gate. Armed with the virtues of humility and greater self-awareness, these travelers stand at the foot of the mountain, ready to begin the ascent. The presence of a guide can make the difference between success and failure and few guides are as well equipped as John of the Cross. This will become more evident in the next chapters. But, before continuing, take time to review your own journey by reflecting on the questions on the next page.

JOURNALING QUESTIONS

1. In what ways have you encountered disillusionment?
2. What interior conflicts did it pose?
3. What was your external response?
4. Did your interior responses differ from your external response? If so, how?
5. Looking back, what were some of the lessons you learned?
6. Do you have a spiritual director?
7. If not, are you motivated to find one? What steps will you take to do so?
8. In the absence of the availability of a formal spiritual guide, who or what might be a suitable substitute?

CHAPTER IV

THE FOOT OF THE MOUNTAIN

BEGINNING THE JOURNEY

Despite the fact that they have been journeying for a while, John of the Cross would regard those who have experienced romance and disillusionment as beginners on the spiritual path. Now, these spiritual travelers leave sensory satisfaction behind and enter what he calls "the dark night."

I find that the term "dark night" has been overused in recent times, and even misused. It has become part of the spiritual lexicon used to describe difficulties encountered in the spiritual life and, unfortunately, the focus is all too negative. John of the Cross maintains that the dark night is an important part of the journey to union with God and, therefore, is not only positive, but necessary. What John calls the dark night has been described as the purgative way as early as the third century. But unless we understand the tremendous grace that is hidden in the darkness, the focus remains on enduring rather than on embracing this night.

Whether the purification process is recognized as the dark night is not as important as the desire to seek God who is beckoning in the darkness. In the end, it comes down to a choice. Consequently, beginners who stand at the foot of the mountain are faced with the decision as to whether to begin the ascent or remain where they feel most comfortable.

At this stage, the way of the active apostolate and the contemplative path seem distant and removed from one another. Those journeying on one path may not even notice the other, or if they do, it may be with a sense of near disdain, each believing their path to be the more enlightened way. Therefore, the first step will entail eradicating the presumption that either understands the ways of God. If these sojourners are serious about living for God alone, then they must begin by seeking to know God, which means leaving behind previous misconceptions and entering the night of the unknown.

Why would anyone choose a path that runs contrary to human nature? The answer is simple. When we accept Jesus' invitation to follow Him, other interests lose their attraction. The more we shed other loves and enter into our own poverty, the more content we become and the closer we are to God. When we accept our poverty in peace, expecting nothing from ourselves, we turn more and more to the One who satisfies our deepest need.

Having been brought low through disillusionment, these ministers now long for something more. Realizing their own poverty, they enter what Merton called "the door to freedom." And where there is freedom, there are choices. Poverty of spirit enables spiritual persons to trust the unknown as the way to God. And to choose the way of the unknown is to enter the dark night of sense.

Since John of the Cross has been referred to as the "Doctor of the Dark Night," his approach will be the primary guide as we examine the path to union for ministers. From time-to-time, insights gleaned from the writings of St. Teresa of Avila and others will also be cited to confirm or support the position of the Carmelite friar. Both John and Teresa have long been regarded as models for the contemplative path, but their wisdom also serves as a guide for those who are called to the active apostolate. While not everyone is called to live the charisms of Carmelite spirituality, the principles outlined by these saints resonate with a wider audience than is generally imagined. Therefore, all who seek a deeper relationship with God stand to benefit from their insight.

TERESA AND JOHN

For those who are not familiar with the lives of John and Teresa, a few words about them may prove helpful. Both saints experienced the highest levels of union with God, yet neither Teresa nor John can be looked upon as mountaintop mystics. Within the context of very busy lives, these saints scaled the heights of union and were gifted with the ability to describe the interior journey in ways that lead the way for others. And yet their approaches were as different as the circumstances of their lives.

John was born into poverty. Teresa was a daughter of privilege. Teresa was outgoing. John was inclined toward a more solitary life. Still, he never shunned people. During his early years, John worked in a hospital caring for the sick. After his ordination, he longed to commit himself to a deeper life of prayer, but when Teresa invited him to join her in reforming the Carmelite order, he sacrificed his personal aspirations to embrace the work at hand. In the midst of tremendous obstacles, which eventually resulted in John's being imprisoned by the friars of his own order, he found union with God.

Teresa, who founded seventeen houses of contemplative prayer, was actively involved with matters beyond the convent walls. The securing of property and buildings for the houses she established took a great deal of time and energy. Her critics were numerous and many wished she would simply disappear behind the convent walls for good. While a less active life may have been Teresa's personal preference, she chose to do what she believed was God's will for her. And, in the process, her experience of God brought her into the spiritual marriage. Rather than serving as an escape, her deeply intimate relationship with God contributed to her being a practical and determined reformer.

Traveling through sixteenth century Spain was no easy task. The story is told of Teresa falling into a mud puddle after the wagon she was traveling in overturned. Known for her quick wit and sense of humor, the saint responding by directing her irritation at God and said, "If this is the way you treat your friends, it's no wonder you have so few." Stories like this remind us how human the saints were and that they encountered the same, if not worse, obstacles than ministers today.

At a time when many are disillusioned with the Church because of the sexual abuse scandal, questionable financial practices and hierarchical authority, we would do well to remember these two Carmelite saints. During one of the Church's darkest periods, they reformed their order's way of life and developed a spirituality that resonated with lay people as well as religious. They were scrutinized by the Spanish inquisitors yet, against tremendous odds, they continued the work to which they felt called. Through it all, they became saints and Doctors of the Church.

Upon reaching the spiritual marriage, Sts. John and Teresa reflected on the path they had traveled and, by means of their writings, left behind what serves as a road map for the interior journey. Their insights about prayer and the spiritual life have served the Church through the ages and today their popularity extends far beyond the Catholic audience for which they were intended. Each saint illustrates the uniqueness of a journey which reflects their personalities and their relationship with God. Rather than contradict one another, their descriptions complement each other. Taken together, they provide a landscape of the soul that guides all those who long to be united with the One who longs for union with each soul.

Over the years, John's metaphor of the dark night and Teresa's metamorphosis of the caterpillar into a butterfly have become common language for the Christian journey, validating the universality of their message. The insight of these humble sixteenth century mystics remains relevant for people of all walks of life, especially those in lay ecclesial ministry, whose commitment to the Church is not so different from the saints of long ago.

Teresa wrote for her nuns but also under obedience to her spiritual directors. Her *Interior Castle* is a treatise about the inner sanctum of the soul where God dwells. She uses the image of a castle made of diamond or very clear crystal which has many mansions or dwelling places through which the person travels as the soul responds to the Lord's invitation. The journey to union, if God wills it, and the individual response to grace culminates in the seventh mansion, where the soul is fully united with God.

Teresa's treatment of what God accomplishes in those who are disposed to his grace offers a rare glimpse of the footprint that God leaves in the soul as it journeys toward union. As the saint pointed out,

> We always hear about what a good thing prayer is and our constitution obliges us to spend many hours in prayer, Only what we ourselves can do in prayer is

explained; little is explained about what the Lord does in the soul, I mean about the supernatural.

Her statement illustrates that she was always eager to move beyond the humble efforts of human beings and give credit to God for that which only God can accomplish. This is a trait that ministers who wish to be centered in God must also acquire.

John's work, on the other hand, took the form of poetry. It was written as an outpouring of love describing what his soul had experienced. The nuns with whom he shared his original work were not able to interpret it, and so they prevailed upon him to explain in prose what his heart had given voice to in poetic verse. Today the writings of John of the Cross and Teresa of Avila are numbered among the great spiritual classics and are counted among the greatest works in Spanish literature.

John's poem, *The Dark Night* offers a concise and systematic approach to union with God, albeit through symbol and verse. Nonetheless, it provides an unparalleled formula for the spiritual journey. The first two stanzas of the poem have to do with the purgation a person passes through during both the night of sense and the night of spirit. Stanzas three to eight have to do with the transforming effects experienced by the soul in the illuminative and unitive stages.

When reading John's poem, it is important to understand that the saint penned it after reaching union with God. He offers what could be described as a perspective through a rear view mirror. Having traversed the difficult terrain, he stands atop Mount Carmel (figuratively speaking) and looks back with heartfelt gratitude for all that he encountered along the way. He understands that every crevasse, every jagged edge, indeed the very night that enveloped him, was vital to the ascent. Aware that much of the journey was beyond his power to accomplish or control, John alludes to the peace that was present even during his darkest hours. In retrospect, he calls all of God's work a grace, pulling and lifting him to heights which would be impossible to scale by human effort alone.

Like so many people who have looked back on life situations only to realize that God had been present all along, John's heart overflowed with wonder and gratitude for his nocturnal crises. From the point of departure into the night which culminated at the summit of mystical union, John offers insights that serve as directives for those who feel the tug deep within their being to scale the mountain of God.

John's use of the word "night" is more than a symbol. The dark night was a phenomenon that enveloped him, obscuring all that the senses had come to rely upon. Unable to see beyond the present moment, John relied solely on God. He placed his trust in God, much the way a blind person trusts a seeing-eye dog to lead the way when darkness is all that is known. When the senses no longer guided John, faith and hope became his guides.

Over the years, critics of John of the Cross have accused him of being obsessed with the negative aspects of the spiritual life. His preference for the least and the lowest and his desire for nothing baffles some. But to dismiss the "Doctor of Nada" as irrelevant simply reflects a lack of understanding. Rather than possessing nothing, John possessed everything. "Solo Dios," God alone, is a far more descriptive emblem for the saintly man who understood that when we have God, we have everything.

Not unlike Francis of Assisi who embraced poverty as his "Lady," John embraced the darkness with the tenderness of a lover. He understood that to embrace the night was to imitate Christ crucified in His darkest hour. John immersed himself in the One who cried out, "My God, my God why have you forsaken me" (Mt 27:45), and in so doing, experienced the splendor of the Triune God. In losing himself, John found his identity as a true son of God as he and Jesus, the Bridegroom of his soul, became one.

The more time I spend with the humble friar's poetry, the more it speaks to me. John's poetry helps direct my gaze inward in the midst of demands and duties that are part of the active apostolate. I believe the words of this holy man can guide ministers who stand at the foot of the mountain.

When the night beckons, my advice is to allow John to be your guide. Trust that the depth of grace that awaits you in the darkness of faith will carry you through. If you feel the night approaching, do not be afraid. Should you feel as though the night is devouring you, be assured that faith is the hidden light that will illumine your path. And in the process your heart will be purified until at last your only desire will be that your will and the will of God be made one.

Read the mystic's words thoughtfully and prayerfully. Come back to them often as you continue your journey and allow the cloud of unknowing that fills the nighttime skies to enkindle hope, provide support and inspire a heartfelt desire to scale the mountain of God.

The Dark Night

1. One dark night,
fired with love's urgent longings
-ah the sheer grace!-
I went out unseen,
My house being now all stilled;

2. In darkness and secure,
by the secret ladder, disguised,
- ah, the sheer grace!-
in darkness and concealment,
my house being now all stilled.

3. On that glad night,
in secret for no one saw me,
nor did I look at anything,
with no other light or guide
than the one that burned in my heart.

4. This guided me
more surely than the light of noon
to where he waited for me
- him I knew so well –
in a place where no one else appeared.

5. O guiding night!
O night more lovely than the dawn!
O night that has united
the Lover with his beloved,
transforming the beloved in her Lover.

6. Upon my flowering breast
which I kept wholly for him alone,
there he lay sleeping,
and I caressing him
there in a breeze from the fanning cedars.

7. When the breeze blew from the turret,
as I parted his hair,
it wounded my neck
with its gentle hand,
suspending all my senses.

8. I abandoned and forgot myself,
laying my face on my Beloved;
all things ceased; I went out from myself,
leaving my cares
forgotten among the lilies.

THE UNIVERSAL CALL TO UNION

If you feel intimidated by the saint's profound experience, I encourage you to set aside such temptations. John would be the first to urge all to seek contemplation, the divine gift received as one's relationship with God becomes more intimate. Rather than excluding active apostles, I believe that contemplation is even more important for those who labor in the vineyard of the Lord. Recall the invitation of Jesus, "Come to me all you who labor and are burdened and you shall find rest to your souls." (Mt 11:28)

There is nothing exclusive about the Lord's invitation. If anything it seems to focus especially on those who are prone to action. Those who minister out of love for God will gradually discover their home in the heart of God. It is the reward for those who are single-minded enough to embrace their Christian vocation without reservation. Conversely, those who rest in God's love as their first call will eventually desire to share with the Body of Christ the fruits of their contemplation.

In drawing from the wisdom of the mystics, those who have begun the journey to God through ministry will simply be responding to their soul's deepest yearning which is to know, love and serve God with their whole heart and soul. The journey is mystical and marvelous, treacherous and terrible. But, for those whose hearts have been set ablaze by the Holy Spirit, nothing is impossible. Be assured, we have it on good authority that, "[f]ired by love's urgent longings, souls begin the ascent toward Mystery surrounded by sheer grace!"

JOURNALING QUESTIONS

1. What is my heart's deepest desire?
2. Do I feel drawn to it, or does fear make me want to turn away?
3. What about it frightens me the most?
4. Do I believe God can help me overcome my fear?
5. What role has quiet prayer played in my life?
6. How do I feel when I place myself at the foot of the mountain?
7. Do I equate affective prayer with feelings of consolation?

Part II
The Night of the Senses

CHAPTER V

MORTIFICATION OF THE SENSES

ACTIVE AND PASSIVE NIGHT

Beginning the ascent toward union is synonymous with entering the dark night of sense. As one journeys toward greater intimacy with God, the nights of sense and spirit serve as graced processes that are to be embraced rather than avoided. But in order to embrace them, it helps to know something about this nocturnal journey. The night of sense precedes the night of the spirit and is experienced on a physical, intellectual and emotional level. The night of spirit, which includes the capacity for love and knowledge, pertains to the deeper, more interior dimension of the human person.

John of the Cross further categorizes the nights of sense and spirit according to active and passive dispositions. He describes the person's active participation in the spiritual journey in *The Ascent of Mount Carmel* and that which God accomplishes in the soul within the darkness in *The Dark Night*. However, the active and passive nights are so closely intertwined that at times one is scarcely distinguishable from the other. They could be likened to two coils of a single rope, tightly twisted around each other. The twisted rope is analogous to the alternating initiative between God and the spiritual seeker who journeys toward union with God. At times one puts forth tremendous effort, and then there are periods where God seems to lift the soul over terrain it could not traverse on its own. By means of alternating active and passive night experiences, the soul is strengthened and purified. And so it happens that the more effort a person puts forth, the more enlightened the soul becomes in the ways of God, and the more a person is gradually transformed into the image of God.

The purpose of the dark night, according to John, is three-fold. The first pertains to the mortification of the senses, the second has to do with the obscurity of journeying in faith and the third is related to God's hidden communication in the soul. These actions, which are both human and divine, purify the soul and prepare it for God's illuminating presence and for union with God.

This chapter will explore John's teachings about the mortification of the senses, which today we might refer to as self-discipline, and examine how they apply to active ministry. The succeeding chapters will explore the saint's teachings about journeying in faith and God's hidden communication in ministry.

PURIFICATION OF THE SENSES

To warn those who cling to consolations in prayer about the danger of being led by sensory satisfaction, John of the Cross wrote: "The appetites are like a cataract on the eye or specks of dust in it; until removed they obscure the vision."[1] Recall Jesus' lament that many have eyes to see but do not see. If one is to begin the journey to union, the soul must first be purified of sensory attachments that obscure a person's vision.

John insists that those who are serious about prayer must move beyond consolations. The same holds true for those in active ministry. While we refer to ministry as a supernatural calling, it is lived out in a physical setting and therefore is subject to all the temptations present in any job. Ambition, envy and attachment to personal goals often compete with charity, compassion and poverty of spirit. When the pleasure principle gains mastery over the will, the minister's focus shifts from the true God to lesser gods. Therefore, those who aspire to become lay ecclesial ministers centered in God must follow the way of detachment. They must leave behind self-centered aspirations which conflict with an ever deepening relationship with God. In the following passage, John explains why this is so:

> All the being of creatures compared with the infinite being of God is nothing... therefore, a person attached to creatures is nothing in the sight of God, and even less than nothing, because love causes equality and likeness and even brings the lover lower than the object of its love.[2]

Right from the start, John argues that we must become like that which we love. Therefore, if we are to become like God in whose image we are created, we must set aside disordered attachments. Not only does the saint regard these attachments as obstacles that distract the soul from God, but he views them as the cause of personal misery. As the saint explained, inordinate appetites "weary, torment, darken, defile and weaken" the soul.[3]

Nevertheless, the saint is not suggesting that we reject the senses altogether. The senses are vital. They serve as gateways to human experience and even survival. John understands this. Still, he maintains that we must move beyond sensory satisfaction lest we become imprisoned by its insatiable appetite. He further points out that mortifying the senses does not mean we place ourselves in harms way. He wisely wrote:

> [t]he ignorance of some is extremely lamentable; they burden themselves with extraordinary penances and many other exercises, thinking these are sufficient for the attainment of union with divine wisdom...If these people would devote only half that energy to the renunciation of their desires, they would profit more in a month than in years with all these other exercises.[4]

John's counsel could be summarized with the saying "common sense goes a long way." The process of eating offers one such example. Eating is necessary, natural and contributes to good health. But when we overeat because we enjoy a particular food or meal, our stomach is forced to accommodate the surplus, even resulting in some discomfort. If overeating becomes habitual, the stomach expands and requires more food to produce a feeling of fullness. Over time, eating more than is necessary leads to overweight, which eventually contributes to health problems.

But those who follow the other extreme and deprive their body of adequate nourishment also put their health at risk. Appetites, while good in themselves, must be well ordered. Unless we control our appetites, they will control us. When sensory gratification dictates our behavior, we engage in a form of idolatry since that which we are seeking becomes the object of our heart's desire.

In writing about prayer, John invites those who have depended on consolations or favorite prayer aids, ranging from statues to personal preferences for devotions, to set them aside. Preoccupation with material things or consolations, even those pertaining to the spiritual life, can become obstacles to a deeper relationship with God. Letting go and allowing God to lead are key and require self-discipline as the soul continues to direct its gaze toward the God of consolation rather than toward the consolations of God.

At times God may take the lead, causing souls to experience dryness and aridity, even a dislike for prayer. God leads these persons into the desert so that they may experience inner poverty. Like the Israelites who longed for the "fleshpots of Egypt" while in the desert, persons of prayer must learn to relinquish sensory satisfaction to appreciate the heavenly manna that God longs to give. Unlike the leeks and onions that tantalized their palates while enslaved in Egypt, manna was bland by comparison. Still, as the chosen people gathered the heavenly food, they learned to depend on God for sustenance and not simply on their own efforts.

Like those who travel the path of prayer, ministers are also invited to let go of sensory satisfaction so they can begin their ascent. Some would argue that those who decide to enter lay ecclesial ministry, either as volunteers or paid staff, are already mortifying their senses. After all, volunteers are donating time and energy that could be spent in more pleasurable activities. Those who enter lay ecclesial ministry as a profession do so knowing their income will be less than many who may have less education and perform for less work. Consequently, money or selfishness is rarely viewed as an obstacle. Yet, for some, resentment about low salaries or no salary, in the case of volunteers, can creep in and become an obstacle to the spiritual life.

• • •

Ken, a psychotherapist, had been facilitating wellness workshops as a way to supplement his income. After retiring at age fifty-five, he took a position with the diocesan Office of Spiritual Formation. Since his new position involved using some of the material he had previously developed for workshops, he found himself being "creative" using his contacts within the diocese to further the business he continued to maintain on the side. Eventually, this posed a conflict of interest and he was informed by his supervisor that the proceeds from the workshops should go to the Office of Spiritual Formation. Ken was indignant and secretly found a way to work around this.

Although he had been able to rationalize his actions, it took time and energy to conceal what he was doing. Before long, Ken began experiencing an uneasiness that he realized was caused by his lack of honesty. As he weighed the money he was receiving from his outside business against his peace of mind, he decided it was not worth it. Once he stopped withholding the money from the diocese, not only did Ken regain his peace of mind, but he was able to prepare for the workshops during office hours. Not only did Ken have greater peace of mind, but his time at home became his own. In letting go of the desire for recognition beyond his work for the Church and for what he viewed as extra income, Ken could approach God more openly. He had removed what had become a stumbling block to his relationship with God, and his inner peace was restored.

• • •

Recall that when the rich young man asked Jesus what he must do to inherit eternal life, Jesus responded by telling him to keep the commandments. But when the man insisted he had done this from his youth, Jesus told him that if he wished to be perfect he must sell what he had, give the money to the poor and follow him.

Keeping the commandments is a minimalist attitude. But union with God requires the dedication of our entire being to follow the highest good. Therefore, it should come as no surprise that a lack of detachment prevents people of faith from making progress in the spiritual life. The teaching of Jesus validates St. John's observation that God cannot fill an occupied heart.

As difficult as letting go of disordered attachments may seem, it is the only way to experience freedom from the bondage of sin, the type of freedom that leads to true happiness. In choosing God over self, we are spared the lot of the young man, who Scripture tells us went away sad.

THE DEMONS WITHIN

Sensory desires often operate on an unconscious level. Like the serpent in the Garden of Eden, vices often masquerade as a seeming good. Therefore, it is important to pay attention to what attracts us and what repels us, and understand the reason why.

A regular examination of conscience and prayerful reflection regarding the underlying motives of behavior can shed light on ulterior motives which might otherwise go undetected. Natural inclinations often appear innocent, but temptation and hidden dangers elude those who are less than vigilant. The urge to talk about the faults of others, to judge their motives or defend ourselves at the expense of someone else may seem harmless and even justified at times, but they are nevertheless a sin against charity. The more we allow ourselves to sit quietly in prayer and listen to God speak to our heart, the more we become aware of our failings in this regard and of God's mercy and loving invitation to follow Him alone.

• • •

When the new pastor arrived at St. Mary's, Janice and Terry had a difficult time adapting to his leadership style. They found him controlling and within months of his arrival were making disparaging remarks about him. When they were together, they inevitably found themselves discussing his management techniques, which only seemed to fuel their discontent. They referred to the gripe sessions as therapy but they were anything but therapeutic.

After attending a retreat, Terry decided they needed to manage their discontent in a more constructive manner. A friend who was a therapist suggested that she and Janice have lunch with her to learn how to deal with conflict in a more constructive manner. During the course of the conversation, they learned how they could be assertive and yet respectful. They learned how to share their concerns without being critical or attacking the pastor's approach. In the process, they discovered their pastor was more open than they had previously realized. As a result, not only did their resentment dissipate, their relationship with their pastor improved. The experience taught them that the only behavior they could change was their own, and that when they changed their own behavior, it had a domino effect on the behavior of others.

• • •

A pastoral council chairperson once told me that the real meetings took place in the parking lot after the official meeting was over. The business of the meeting was rehashed as people paired off and lingered, discussing what had taken place with people who saw things as they did. Comments that people would not make about someone face-to-face were freely made behind their back. This type of divisive behavior added to the tension. Some month later, the pastor invited a professional from outside the parish to facilitate a community building retreat. During the weekend experience, members came to know one another and were able to move beyond the differences that had divided them in the past.

• • •

Opting for charity may not always be the popular choice but eventually it leads to a win-win situation. For example, at an interfaith meeting that included a number of clergy and church professionals from several denominations, the discussion turned to a project that had been suggested by a member who was absent that day. When a few people began criticizing and second-guessing the absent person's motives for suggesting the project, one of the rabbis spoke up and said, "I'm not comfortable talking about him since he's not here." It was enough to prick everyone's conscience and, needless to say, we moved on to the next item on the agenda.

࿇ • • • ࿇

Sin wounds the community but it also contributes to the sinner's personal misery. Comparing the practice of giving in to one's natural inclinations to an itch that a person continues to scratch, St. Bernard of Clairvaux wrote:

> [p]leasure turns to pain and agony follows itching. While the man was scratching he ignored the consequences, although he knew what would happen. In the same way we have lacerated ourselves and given ulcers to our unhappy souls with our own hands – except that in a spiritual creature it is more serious because its nature is finer and so more difficult to mend.[5]

Though good in themselves, the senses become obstacles to union with God when they have free reign. Detachment presumes self-knowledge and we typically learn the most about ourselves when things go contrary to expectations.

In his book *The Return of the Prodigal Son,* Henri Nouwen offered a personal example of this phenomenon.[6] The author pointed out that his mood was often linked to the way others viewed him. When his talks were well received, his mood was up, but when he encountered a less than enthusiastic reception or criticism, it quickly came crashing down. Being aware of his interior reaction to external triggers turned out to be a watershed moment for the renowned speaker. He attributed his eventual decision to live and work as pastor at L'Arche Society Daybreak to this personal discovery. He realized that the residents at L'Arche were not impressed by his accomplishments, nor did they esteem him as a renowned speaker. To them he was simply "Henri." They regarded him as one of them, which eliminated any inclination toward pretense.

SEVEN CAPITAL VICES

The demons that lurk within are rooted in the vices of pride, avarice, anger, envy, lust, gluttony and sloth. Exposing their presence and overcoming the power they exert over us is part of the spiritual journey. This is not always easy. Some are obvious while others operate in a more subtle manner.

Take the perfectionist who spends an inordinate amount of time doing and re-doing activities in order to appear flawless. Feeding this type of compulsion extracts more time and energy then is necessary or healthy. Then, there are those with poor self-esteem who participate in church ministry as a way to validate personal worth. In the process they become what they do, clinging to a role or a title which, in their mind, affirms their self-worth. Ministers who chase after success, praise or admiration head down a dead-end as praise is short-lived and yesterday's accolades are quickly forgotten.

Monitoring interior responses to both positive and negative situations can teach those in ministry a great deal about the inner demons that drive behavior. Assessing and humbly accepting personal limitations without worrying how they will be judged frees ministers from feelings of misplaced guilt that may otherwise accompany saying "no."

Jesus' lament that the harvest is plentiful but the laborers are few is not to be interpreted that ministers must personally take on every request or respond to every need that comes their way. People pleasers or those who feel they have to do it all stand to learn something about interior motives from the parable of the ten maidens in Matthew's Gospel (Mt 25:1-13).

In this parable, Jesus offers a healthy and holy approach to mission and ministry. Recall that ten maidens took their lamps and went to meet the bridegroom. Five were wise since they took additional oil with them, but the five foolish maidens brought only the oil that was in their lamps. As they awaited the arrival of the bridegroom, they all fell asleep. When the bridegroom's arrival was announced, the lamps of the foolish maidens were almost dry so they asked the wise maidens to give them some of their oil. Their request was refused. Much to their surprise, they were told to go to the suppliers to buy oil for their lamps. When they returned, they found the banquet door had been closed and they were not allowed to enter.

A common reaction when first hearing the parable is to view the wise maidens as selfish for not sharing their oil. But a closer look reveals that the wise maidens never lost sight of their mission. Their concern was to provide light for the wedding feast. They were not concerned that others might judge them harshly. They were realistic and knew their oil supply was limited. They had enough oil for the mission but no more. Had they shared what they had with the foolish maidens, all ten lamps would have run dry and the wedding hall would be left in darkness. It is a classic example of the adage, "your lack of planning need not become my emergency," unless of course we allow it to be so.

The parable offers lay ministers food for thought since hidden needs and motives can sidetrack ministers and lead to discouragement or failure. The foolish maidens represent those who through procrastination or poor planning create crises that need not occur. When human weakness gains mastery over the will, sensory appetites control behavior and become not only obstacles to the spiritual life but impede the fruitfulness of one's efforts.

• • •

Jake, a minister of Justice and Peace, experienced this first-hand. When he began his ministry, he was enthusiastic and compassionate. He was committed to his work, but over time his zeal was turning him into an angry and sometimes cynical person. He was going to two and three meetings a day and rarely had time to spend with his family, who were beginning to resent his work. In the process Jake was becoming a self-made martyr. When others refused his requests for help, Jake re-doubled his efforts, thinking he could shame them into reconsidering. As a result, the people he was trying to recruit began avoiding him. He alienated those he was called to empower. Jake's over-extended behavior brought him to the point of exhaustion. Self-righteous thinking soon turned to resentment and, as a result, he found little joy in his ministry. And yet much of his suffering was of his own making.

• • •

John of the Cross addressed a similar tendency which shows a lack of Christian maturity. In discussing pride in beginners on the spiritual journey, the saint wrote they condemn others who do not seem to have the kind of devotion they would like them to have, and sometimes gives expression to this criticism like the Pharisee who despised the publican while he boasted and praised God for the good deeds he himself had accomplished.[7]

Needing to be appreciated or overreaching one's capabilities can lead to physical exhaustion and emotional stress. Headaches, high blood pressure, insomnia, fatigue, overeating or loss of appetite can be job related. Negative emotions such as resentment, anger, cynicism, shame, guilt or depression can also be work-related and, when left unchecked, lead to burnout and can even cause an emotional breakdown. Some become so embittered, they leave the Church. Ministers who procrastinate, avoid unpleasant tasks, engage in self-righteous thinking or manipulate others intensify their own suffering. Giving in to natural inclinations through blaming, judging or condemning intensifies stress and distances the soul from the One who calls us to love.

Over concern about how they are perceived by others is another pitfall that ministers can fall. Since most ecclesial ministers are educated in theology or a related field, they are often looked to as an authority figure. But ministry is about more than having the right answers. Ministers can lose sight of the fact that wisdom and the possession of information do not necessarily go hand-in-hand. In the absence of humility, being esteemed by others can actually be a trap.

John of the Cross addressed this phenomenon regarding prayer, and a similar analogy can be drawn regarding ministry. "Therefore, in their desire to appear holy, they enjoy relating their good behavior to their confessor, and in such careful terms that these good deeds appear greater than they actually are."[8] He goes on to explain that while they enjoy being praised, they dislike praising others and are often uncomfortable when others are esteemed. Basking in spotlight or being regarded as an expert on a particular topic can become an obstacle in our relationship with God. Ministers who lap up compliments like a cat licking a bowl of cream do so at great spiritual risk. Being "on stage" becomes its own reward, and Satan loves nothing better than to thwart the spiritual progress of those who have devoted their life to furthering the Kingdom of God.

A MORE ENLIGHTENED WAY

One way to counter this temptation is by being attentive to the gifts that God has given others. This practice serves as an antidote for inflated egos while empowering others. Ministers who support and encourage others strengthen the Body of Christ, build community, and in the process lighten their own load. By deflecting their own importance and focusing on others, ministers experience the reciprocal dimension of their vocation. And in the absence of affirmation, ministers can take heart in the words of St. Francis of Assisi, "It is in giving that we receive, it is in pardoning that we are pardoned and it is in dying that we are born to eternal life."[9]

Death has many forms. In dying to the desire for sensory gratification, ministers are blessed with a deeper understanding and appreciation for the presence of God in their midst. Sometimes it is difficult to know where our efforts leave off and God's grace begins. But the reality is that one is bathed in the other. The dark night does not mean that we sit by passively, give up or expect God to perform miracles. It means that we own our limitations and work with the grace that is present within the darkness. Ministers, like those who travel the path of prayer, can benefit from the advice of John of the Cross who wrote:

> To reach satisfaction in all, desire its possession in nothing.
> To come to possess all, desire the possession of nothing.
> To arrive at being all, desire to be nothing.
> To come to the knowledge of all, desire the knowledge of nothing.
> To come to the pleasure you have not, you must go by a way you enjoy not.
> To come to the knowledge you have not, you must go by a way in which you possess not.

When you turn toward something, you cease to cast yourself upon the all.[10]

The purgative way, though initially distasteful, cleanses the soul and ultimately frees it, opening it to God's action within. In stripping away disordered attachments, God heals the soul, further predisposing it to accept the graces hidden within each moment. Spiritual insights and the presence of virtue are the external fruits of the wisdom and inner peace by which God enriches these souls. Whether acquired through ministry or in prayer, wisdom goes hand in hand with self-knowledge. When ministers realize how easily the senses distort and lead them astray, they find God by spending time seeking his presence within. As God continues to draw them toward the divine dwelling place, ministers, like persons who began the journey on the path of prayer, learn to trust the darkness and walk by faith. Along the way, contemplatives begin to view the world through a more apostolic lens, for how can one take on the heart of Christ without taking on His body? In a similar manner, ministers become more committed to deepening their relationship with God through prayer.

JOURNALING QUESTIONS

1. What are sources of joy, frustration and anxiety in your ministry?
2. Which of the following are most apt to dissipate your energy?
   Disappointment   Rejection   Criticism   Failure
3. What is your usual manner of responding to these experiences?
4. What behavior patterns hinder your recovery?
5. What behavior patterns assist your recovery?

CHAPTER VI

JOURNEYING IN FAITH

TRUSTING THE DARKNESS

As indicated in chapter five, the second purpose of the dark night according to John of the Cross has to do with journeying in faith. Since faith requires trust, God leads persons at this stage by depriving them of the clarity and certitude that marked their spiritual journey during an earlier time. John offers the following insights about what is taking place and the reason why this is so:

> Consequently, it is at this time they are going about their spiritual exercises with delight and satisfaction, when in their opinion the sun of divine favor is shining most brightly on them, that God darkens all this light and closes the door and the spring of the sweet spiritual water they were tasting as often and as long as they desired. For since they were weak and tender, no door was closed to them.[1]

This deprivation leads to feelings of such anxiety that those brought to this night are not sure where to turn. The natural instinct is to try to make suffering end, but John counsels those who wish to make progress in prayer to abandon themselves to God so that their faith may be strengthened. It seems that God strengthens ministers by means of a similar nocturnal experience. As those in the active apostolate deal with constraints of time and resources, often juggling responsibilities at home, or in the case of volunteers, at work, some things may go undone. Ministers can easily feel overwhelmed. This may lead to discouragement, inadequacy or feelings of ambivalence. Others may become frustrated or angry, while still others may develop a martyr's complex or exhibit a lack of patience with people who make demands on their time. All of the above are telling signs that go beyond disillusionment and are often associated with impending burnout.

Such symptoms are regarded as natural phenomena. They are equated with stress but are often rooted in pride and a false sense of self-sufficiency. Like a loving parent, God desires to teach ministers at this stage that human effort is not enough. He leads them by way of the passive night, taking them where they are unwilling or unable to go on their own. In the midst of this type of darkness, a deliberate and conscious effort to walk by faith is needed for further growth. Therefore the encouragement of a spiritual director is particularly important during this stage.

Spiritual directors who support struggling ministers with compassion and understanding can help direct their gaze away from themselves toward a more God-centered approach. An experienced spiritual guide herself, St. Teresa expressed compassion for those who were still in the beginning stages of this dark night when she wrote:

> I have found neither a way of consoling nor a cure for such persons other than to show them compassion in their affliction – and, indeed compassion is felt on seeing them subject to such misery – and not contradict their reasoning. For everything in their minds leads them to think they are suffering these things for God, and so, they don't come to realize that their disturbance is an imperfection. [2]

At a time when personal resolve seems to languish, a spiritual guide must be sensitive to the struggle, even as they encourage the minister to embrace in faith that which reason tends to question. Consequently, directors play a pivotal role in helping beginners value this lack of clarity as the path to a more proficient and eventually more perfect way of being with God. This night is the means by which persons who love God are being drawn into the Paschal Mystery as a lived experience and not simply as a profession of faith. In time, they will come to value the darkness as a source of hope rather than a cause for despair, but usually only after it has passed.

In prayer, these trials are referred to as the desert; in ministry they are viewed as the cross. That which was once a source of assurance and consolation now seems to be stale and tedious. Just as persons of prayer believe they are doing something wrong and may be tempted to return to a previous form of prayer, so ministers question their ability to function effectively. When efforts result in an emotionally less satisfying experience, ministers, like those on the path of prayer, are invited to believe that God continues to lead them and, thus, they must persevere. This is a time for beginners to rely more on God and less on their own ability. Those who had previously been very action-oriented must now learn to spend time simply being with God.

At times, this seems to be a waste of time, particularly when minds keep returning to tasks waiting to be done and phone calls to return. But all the mystics agree that patience and perseverance are essential. St. Edith Stein advised the following:

> They should do absolutely nothing, other than persevere patiently in prayer without any activity what so ever; all that is required of them here is freedom of soul, that they may liberate themselves from the impediment and fatigue of ideas and thoughts, and care not about thinking or meditating. They must be content simply with a loving and peaceful attentiveness to God, and live without concern, without the effort, and without the desire to taste or feel him.[3]

While planning, meetings and projects may garner the greater part of a minister's time, those in the active apostolate must take care to set aside specific time for prayer each day. If the minister's work is to be fruitful, prayer time must be treated as sacred. It must become the anchor that grounds faith and work. Prayer cannot be looked upon as expendable. Ministers who feel guilty because they consider themselves remiss in their duties when they spend time in prayer may find reassurance from the following Scripture passage: "Martha, Martha, you are busy about many things but Mary has chosen the better part and it shall not be taken from her" (Lk 10:41-42). In addition, Jesus tells us this:

> Abide in me as I abide in you. Just as the branch cannot bear fruit of itself unless it abides in the vine, neither can you unless you abide in me. I am the vine, you are the branches. Those who abide in me and I in them, bear much fruit, because apart from me you can do nothing. (Jn 15:4-5)

If progress is to be made, those in the active apostolate must know that prayer is as vital to their ministry as food is to their physical health.

PRACTICAL APPLICATIONS OF TRUSTING GOD

Anita was a morning person and found that she did her best early in the day. She woke up feeling refreshed and often felt the urge to get right to work. However, over the years she learned the importance of personal prayer time. On the days when she gave into the impulse to postpone her prayer time, she discovered she quickly got caught up in the activities of the day. By the time she realized she had not made time for God in prayer, it was late and she was too tired even to try. Further examination helped Anita realize that there was a direct correlation between prayer, the effectiveness of her work, and way she related to people. Beginning her day by centering in God made her a kinder, more patient person. As a result, she made the commitment to spend the first thirty minutes of her day in quiet prayer. As commendable as her commitment may be, those who practice prayer must also examine their motives. If prayer is viewed as a way to achieve serenity or success in their ministry rather than an offering of self to God, those who commit themselves to daily prayer have missed the point. Selfish motives can creep into every aspect of life, even prayer, which make vigilance and ongoing self-examination imperative.

Setting aside time to be with God often requires a huge amount of effort. But many of the saints experienced the same problem. Theresa of Avila wrote that there were days when sitting through the required prayer time felt more like torture than prayer. And St. Therese of Lisieux admitted to falling asleep during prayer. Those who take prayer seriously can take comfort knowing that God looks at our heart and sees our intention. Remaining faithful to the practice of prayer when we do not feel like praying means moving beyond the way a person feels.

To journey in faith means those who pray must learn to trust the darkness. In a culture that prides itself on doing, the idea of doing nothing, even in regard to prayer, may evoke a negative response. But being faithful often means not only depriving the senses, but ignoring logic when faith suggests a different approach. Mother Teresa cautioned that faithfulness rather than success should be the goal for those who wish to serve God. As busy as her life was, Mother Teresa spent two hours before the Blessed Sacrament every morning following Mass. In her journal she explained that she wanted to give Jesus the first part of her day.

Depending on schedules, responsibilities and body clocks, early morning may not suit everyone. The important thing is that you choose a time during the day when there is little chance of being interrupted, and then honor that time as sacred. Every laborer needs time to relax and experience being accepted for who they are rather than for what they can do for others. And ministers are no exceptions. Often this means following the same advice they give others. Ministers must come to know and appreciate who they are in the eyes of God. I recall one minister sharing with me that she wondered if she had any real friends. She felt that when people looked at her, all they saw was a parish minister.

If ministers are completely task-oriented or wear the mask of the busy person, they may be contributing to the sense of isolation they feel. When ministers view those they encounter simply as potential volunteers, they miss an opportunity to establish a meaningful relationship. Focusing on relationships rather than the task at hand helps ministers appreciate their own and each person's true identity as a child of God. The more secure ministers are in their own identity, the better they can respond to others as members of the same family. But self-care does not happen unless ministers make it happen.

• • •

At a regional meeting, a group of ministers complained that it had been years since they had read a book that was not work-related. Since spiritual books are often the tools of the trade, ministers can miss opportunities for growth because their focus is too task-directed. When Paula read the book that the adult formation group was using for discussion during Lent, her focus was on how she would use the material with the group rather than being mindful of how it pertained to her own life. At the suggestion of her spiritual director, she approached the preparation time more prayerfully and was pleasantly surprised how meaningful the time had become for her. What had once been a project for the head became a project of the heart. She found that reading in the chapel and allowing time for reflective prayer rather than sitting in her office made all the difference in the way she approached the project. In setting aside time to listen to what the readings were saying, she discovered a depth of understanding that had been absent when she approached it as though it were one more task to accomplish. As a result, she was able to share on a deeper level with the group and a bond based on genuine friendships evolved.

ꕤ • • • ꕤ

A friend who worked as a minister to the sick set aside one day each month as a "desert day" that was devoted to prayer and spiritual reading. Most ministers discover that the more time they spend in prayer, the more they realize that prayer is not an option but a matter of survival. It serves as a calm amid the storms of life; the lighthouse that calls them home to the heart of God.

TEACH US TO PRAY

When the apostles asked Jesus to teach them how to pray, He taught them the Our Father. It was not that the apostles did not know how to pray. It was the custom of teachers to provide their disciples with a prayer which encompassed their particular philosophy, an emblem of sorts that provided them with an identity. In keeping with this custom, Jesus taught them the Our Father. The prayer captures the essence of Jesus' identity and encapsulates His teachings in a concise and profound manner.

Teresa and John's writings provide a similar paradigm, albeit not as concise. More than an instruction, they provide a view of what it means to live as a true son and daughter of the Father. Yet each provides a unique view of the interior journey. For John, prayer was a way to enter into the presence of God with nothing but the faith, hope and love that guided him. There were no words or images; no book was required. His imprisonment in the monastery at Toledo left him with only his breviary, which he could read only by morning's light if he stood on a stool near the tiny solitary window in his cell. Teresa, on the other hand, rarely approached prayer without a book on her lap. Even if she never opened it, it served as a reminder that reading could jump start her prayer. Her prayer was Christo-centric. Some may consider her approach similar to the practice of "Lectio Divina," which makes use of a Scripture passage or a word by which to enter into prayer. Teresa complained that she did not have the skills required to engage in lengthy discursive meditation. Consequently, she would simply place herself in the Gospel scene and be present to the Lord without saying or thinking about anything. She described her prayer as simply looking in faith at the one present within who loved her.

ꕤ • • • ꕤ

Art's introduction to contemplative prayer began with the rosary. Although he had attended daily Mass most of his life, he became aware of a deepening desire for prayer. He felt the need to do more and decided to pray the rosary on a daily basis. Eventually, this opened the door to contemplative prayer. He chose a time when he knew he would not be disturbed, meditating on the mysteries as he prayed. In the beginning, it would take about ten to fifteen minutes for him to pray five decades of the rosary, but after a few weeks it took longer and longer until he noticed that almost an hour would pass before he finished. Over time, Art would get as far as the fourth mystery and could go no further. He could only rest in the presence of God. Not understanding what was taking place, he found this disturbing. He thought there was something wrong with him because he could not get through five decades of a rosary. But when Art confided his concern to a priest, he was told to read the works of St. Teresa of Avila. That was Art's introduction to contemplative prayer as a gift from God. The point is that there is no one way to approach contemplation. In the Carmelite tradition, contemplation is regarded as infused prayer. It is about God's action in the life of each person. When we dispose ourselves by setting aside time to be faithful to prayer, we open ourselves to receive all that God desires to give us.

• • •

In recent years, there has been a resurgence of interest in quiet prayer which is sometime referred to as centering prayer. This has given rise to numerous books that offer techniques to quiet the mind. The use of a sacred word, or concentrating on one's breath are two approaches often suggested, but there is no best technique. Each person must find what is right for him or her. To be faithful requires believing that putting oneself in the presence of God is prayer regardless of the feelings it may generate.

By owning our inability to advance on our own, we place our trust in God to lead the way. This may explain why John and Teresa spend so little time on method and concentrate on the goal, which is union with God. When we focus on the presence of God within our deepest center, our focus shifts from self to God and prayer becomes a gateway to self-emptying. In the process hearts are purified. More important than methodology is the willingness to be purified of all that stands in the way of a deeper relationship with God. And so we do well to recall Jesus' words, "Blessed are the pure of heart for they will see God" (Mt 5:8).

DARKNESS IN THE MARKETPLACE

The spiritual life does not operate in a vacuum, so it is not surprising that the darkness experienced in prayer is often mirrored in life. A lack of consolation does not mean God has rejected us. In fact, John insists the opposite is true. From a spiritual perspective, we are often at our best when we are most abject. Greater awareness of our own limitations and misery can lead to greater poverty of spirit and a willingness to rely on the Holy Spirit rather than our own efforts.

Nevertheless, a lack of consolation in prayer or ministry should be accompanied by prayerful discernment. Has our prayer or ministry become difficult despite continued effort or have we grown lax? Are we being called to journey more deeply by faith or is this desert, this crisis a result of laziness or avoidance? Vigilance and honest appraisal about our commitment to prayer and work help us discern the reason for the lack of consolation. If the struggle persists despite our best efforts, then it may well be that God is inviting us to deeper levels of trust. The less confident we are about our own ability, the more apt we are to depend on God for divine assistance, not as a substitute but to give leverage to the effort we put forth.

Understanding that God speaks through people and life situations can help ministers be more attentive to how God is leading them during times of darkness. But it can also pose a conundrum for ministers. It may arouse feelings of uncertainty about how or when it is appropriate to disclose personal struggles. Sharing struggles can be helpful. However, if a minister turns to the community that he or she is being called to serve for support or counsel, sharing those struggles would be inappropriate. If the struggle is one that is already known to the community, ministers may ask for prayers. By word and example they can demonstrate how they place their trust in God even as they work toward resolution and deeper trust.

An example of this would be the late Cardinal Bernardin, who when he was accused of sexually abusive behavior, spoke publicly about the accusation. He maintained his innocence but did not actively seek sympathy from the public. He openly proclaimed his trust in God regardless of the outcome and his faith became a source of inspiration for others. For a minister to pretend all is well, when it is obvious to others that they are going through personal difficulties, would be disingenuous.

While community can provide a great support, generally speaking, lay ministers should not seek support from the same community that the minister is serving. Prayer, the Scriptures, a spiritual director or a trusted friend can be a source of support during times of difficulty. In addition, those much-needed delicate touches of grace often come from the most unlikely people.

• • •

A faculty member at a Catholic university shared one such experience with his class. As a student working on his doctoral dissertation, he was advised by his reader to discard the nearly three hundred pages he had written and start over. He was devastated. Being rejected was bad enough, but it also meant that he would have to ask his religious community to extend his sabbatical. Given the declining number of priests, this was no small matter.

Judging himself a failure and feeling completely dejected, he decided to go for a walk. Along the way, a homeless man praising God in a loud voice walked toward him. In an effort to avoid the man, the priest crossed the street. Much to his disappointment, the man did the same. Before he knew it, the man was standing in front of him wanting to know if the priest loved Jesus. When he responded "Yes" the man reached out and touched the priest's shoulder. Looking him in the eye, the man said, "Then you're a good boy." The priest told us that the words and gesture of this homeless man had a profound effect on him. He was affirmed in a way he could not have anticipated but the affirmation gave him the courage to request the time he needed to complete his dissertation.

Encounters with grace need not be dramatic. God works within the context of daily life, but often the presence of God is felt only after the crisis has passed. Yet, every time we trust that God is present in the unknown, faith is strengthened. Then, like a trusted friend, faith becomes a guide, a companion that leads the way to self-emptying and greater intimacy with God. In this way, the active and passive nights work together to lead souls toward divine union.

A DIVINE PARTNERSHIP

The active and passive dimensions of the dark night serve as a model for the delicate partnership between God and the human person in regard to prayer. But this partnership is equally important in ministry. Some things are simply beyond the capability of human beings to accomplish. This is illustrated in the account of the boy who was possessed by an evil spirit in Mark's Gospel.

Jesus was approached by the father of a boy who was possessed. The earlier attempt by the disciples to cast the evil spirit from his son had been unsuccessful. Upon hearing this, Jesus rebuked his disciples for their lack of faith and then directed His attention to the boy. After the boy was cured, the disciples asked Jesus why they had not been able to cast out the demon. Jesus answered "This kind can come out only through prayer" (Mk 9:29).

The account illustrates the point that sometimes good intentions may not be enough. Ministry involves a partnership between God and his people and prayer is the way to deepen that partnership. Prayer must accompany the active apostolate, not merely as a means of intercession but through a union of wills between God and the minister. In the Gospel account, Jesus was clearly disappointed with His disciples. After spending so much time with them, they remained blind to the fact that everything Jesus did was done in union with the Father. If they were to follow His example, they must do the same. The power to exorcize demons, both those within and those encountered in life's situations, must be rooted in the minister's relationship with God. And prayer is the doorway to that relationship.

As was pointed out in a previous chapter, inner demons, which are present in every person, can be the driving force behind good works. They prey on human weakness and captivate the senses, blinding them to the light of God's love. The dark night of sense exposes these demons. Rather than giving in and allowing them to gain mastery, faith invites us to trust that God is indeed guiding us in the midst of suffering, uncertainty and even failure.

To walk by faith requires a delicate balance between action and prayerful listening. Trials and suffering can become the vehicles that strengthen faith. The greater the minister's faith, the greater the capacity to trust God despite circumstances that might suggest otherwise. Thomas Merton, who was both an activist and a contemplative monk, expressed these thoughts in a well-known prayer:

> My Lord God, I have no idea where I am going. I do not see the road ahead of me. I cannot know for certain where it will end. Nor do I really know myself, and the fact that I think I am following your will does not mean that I am actually doing so. But I believe that the desire to please you does in fact please you. And I hope that I will never do anything apart from that desire. And I know that if I do this, you will lead me by the right road, though I may know nothing about it.[4]

Like persons of prayer, ministers are called to abandon the certitude that was present during an earlier stage. Although this night is highly efficacious, the fruits are hidden from these nocturnal pilgrims. And so faith becomes the light in the darkness that strengthens these weary travelers to persevere.

St. Teresa of Avila wrote that prayer and self-indulgence cannot coexist, and we might easily conclude that this also applies to ministry. When the senses fail to sustain, or perhaps because the senses fail to sustain the initial enthusiasm, the decision to proceed rests on the minister's willingness to depend on God. Then God accomplishes that which is beyond human capability.

In the presence of this type of trust, and almost without realizing that a shift is taking place, ministers begin to experience ministry as a seamless garment woven through the love relationship that has its beginning and end in God. Often without understanding why, ministers begin to seek God in new ways as they are drawn more and more toward the path of prayer. As they deepen their own experience of God, the path of those who are led by way of the active apostolate begins to converge with those on the path of prayer.

Similarly, contemplatives discover the prophetic dimension of their vocation. Even those who have been given the special charisma of devoting their life to prayer behind the walls of a cloistered monastery grow into a deeper appreciation of their life as an extension of the Body of Christ whom they are called to serve.

Ministers who may have been critical of the cloistered way of life by viewing it as an escape from the pressures of the world now begin to appreciate its true value. They understand prayer provides the foundation upon which the active apostolate takes root and thrives, even as they begin to value the contemplative path as a necessary part of their own journey toward deeper intimacy with God.

JOURNALING QUESTIONS

1. What role has prayer played in my life in ministry?
2. Does my relationship with God help in ministry?
3. Do I take time to listen to God in prayer and in the events of my life?
4. If not, what am I afraid I might hear?
5. How has God spoken to me during times of uncertainty through people I have encountered?
6. Was I open to their voice?
7. What role does prayer play in my life today?

CHAPTER VII
GOD'S HIDDEN COMMUNICATION

IN THE SECRET OF THE NIGHT

John of the Cross identifies God's hidden communication in the soul as the third purpose of the dark night. He compares this secret communication to air that escapes when one tries to grasp it. Though obscure, it offers a glimpse that there is more to the spiritual journey than was previously imagined. John instructs those who are drawn to contemplative prayer to dispose themselves by quietly opening themselves to God's initiative. Their disposition must remain one of trust as they wait upon God's action in their soul in ways that cannot be seen. In verse one of *The Dark Night* John wrote, "I went out unseen." This represents the liberation of the soul from its former dependency on natural passions and tangible results.

In the beginning stages of contemplation, a person who practices prayer experiences only intense longing for God. As prayer becomes less satisfying, this thirst for God seems to go unrequited and only an experience of dryness remains. But just as dry kindling ignites the log that eventually produces the fire, so this dryness and intense thirst for God will, over time, produce fruits that are so delicate that they often go unnoticed. As persons of prayer rest in the quiet of "unknowing," patience and fortitude begin to take hold from deep within. In the absence of sensory satisfaction, perseverance is rewarded with a certitude that has its origin in God. In trying to understand God's hidden communication and the effect it has on a person's life at this stage of prayer, the power of restorative sleep serves as an illustrative analogy.

People have different internal clocks. Those who are morning people find that by evening their energy has dissipated along with their mental productivity. When people are tired, they tend to be less objective. Problems play over and over in their mind and fatigue takes its toll at day's end. Sooner or later, they realize that getting a good night's sleep is the best course of action. When they awake the next morning, their outlook has improved. Difficulties that seemed insurmountable the night before suddenly appear manageable in the light of day. As a result, people have come to appreciate and rely on the restorative power of sleep. A sleep specialist could explain what is transpiring in the brain while a person is asleep, but the one who is sleeping would be at a loss to do so.

In an equally secretive manner, God is at work in the night of sense. In darkness and uncertainty, the intellect is freed from bondage to the imagination and the senses.

The soul is invigorated in a way not possible when neither the senses, the memory, nor the imagination are in control. During this dark night, the soul is the recipient of important but subtle touches of grace. Just how this takes place is difficult to explain, but like a good night's sleep, this dark night produces positive effects that are realized only after it has passed.

As if awakening from a good night's sleep, God's hidden communication liberates those who take prayer seriously from former attachments. For lay ministers, this means allowing ministry to flow from prayer rather than using prayer to support the active apostolate. Just as those who deprive themselves of sleep become irritable and less productive, so lay ministers who deprive themselves of prayer suffer similar negative consequences. They are prone to irritability and are quick to judge others when reality falls short of their expectations. But those who pray discover a new freedom from concern about how others view them and gradually a task-driven mindset gives way to a more pastoral approach. They understand that no task is more important than the people they encounter in the exercise of ministry on the Church's behalf.

Mother Teresa's commitment to prayer offers an example of the importance of prayer for those in the active apostolate. The saintly nun knew the Missionaries of Charity could not bring Jesus to those they cared for unless they first experienced Jesus in the sacraments and in prayer before the Blessed Sacrament. Lay ministers do not have the benefit of regularly scheduled prayer times, so they must discipline themselves to schedule prayer into their day. As they balance ministerial work with family commitments and in some cases outside jobs, lay ministers may not have large blocks of time for prayer. However, prayer can be done anywhere, anytime. The important thing is simply to do it.

Rising a few minutes early to devote the first minutes of the day to God is one way to insure that prayer is a priority. It sets a tone that is relationship oriented, rather than task- oriented. Arriving a few minutes early for appointments, allowing time alone in the car before going into a meeting or turning off the computer a few minutes before a person arrives for spiritual direction are all ways that invite more God-centered conversation. One minister decided to take time before meals to pray devoutly. It seems like such a small thing. Yet, when we consider how easy it is to rush through grace before meals as a matter of habit rather than as an opportunity to encounter God, the impact can be huge. Every practice, no matter how insignificant, becomes an opportunity for God's hidden communication to take hold when done mindfully. The more we seize those opportunities, the more centered in God we become. As ministers awaken to the presence of God within the context of everyday life, they discover the strength to deal with unpleasant or challenging situations. During this night, anxiety is replaced with newfound trust, past attachments are replaced with wisdom and virtues become more habitual. John explains how this is so.

> In this arid and obscure night the soul undergoes a thorough reform in its imperfections of avarice, in which it coveted various spiritual objects and was never content with any of its spiritual exercises because of the gratification that was derived from them and the covetousness of its appetite. Since it does not obtain the delight it formerly did from its spiritual practices but rather finds them distasteful and laborious, it uses them so moderately that now perhaps it might fail through defect rather than excess. Nevertheless, God usually imparts to those whom He brings into this night the humility and the readiness, even though they feel displeasure, to do what is commanded of them for His sake alone.[1]

Like a seed that draws nutrients from the soil unseen by the human eye, so the soul is purified by God in secret and in darkness. Deprived of sensory consolation, the darkness becomes a conduit of grace. When we operate primarily at the level of sensory pleasure, the senses are in control and are often the motivating force. But when efforts are no longer rewarded in a tangible way, be it in prayer or in ministry, the work at hand becomes more laborious. The desire for satisfaction driven by an attachment to excitement and enthusiasm are replaced by questions and self-doubt. Yet, when ministers in this night remain faithful to their calling and practice complete charity, God rewards their efforts a hundred fold, though perhaps not in the way they expected. As they awaken to the reality of God's presence during what feels like an absence of God, ministers are more inclined to embrace people or situations that were once repugnant on an emotional level. The strength to do this is an example of God's hidden action in the soul. It empowers the recipient to trust that God is at work in unknown ways. Gifted with these graces, they regard themselves as sowers in the Lord's vineyard instead of harvest masters.

With the focus more on God and those they serve, ministers no longer depend on others to confirm their self worth or their calling. Further, because they no longer consider themselves on "center stage," they seek ways to empower others. They may even hide the good works they do so that God alone will reward them. All this is the result of grace, for slowly and unbeknown to them, God is quietly imprinting deep within the hearts of these minister's values and directives that are rooted in humility.

Now blinded by the presence of God's divine light, the soul is no longer fixated on its own needs. Paradoxically, this night seems to shine a spotlight on the soul, causing it to become more aware of its own sinfulness. Not surprisingly, those in this stage of the journey often believe they are slipping backward when, in fact, they are making significant progress in the spiritual life. Faults that had previously gone unnoticed during an earlier stage are now a source of interior pain and remorse.

Humbled by their weakness, they cry out to God for help. Persons at this stage experience a deeper appreciation of the Sacrament of Reconciliation, for frequent, even daily, reception of the Eucharist, and they find themselves devoting more time to personal prayer. With this new awareness, contrite hearts are motivated to live a more God-centered and virtuous life. Experience confirms what John points out regarding the twofold benefit of God's hidden communication: "God will give illumination by bestowing on the soul not only knowledge of its own misery and lowliness but also knowledge of His grandeur and majesty."[2] Having experienced the effects of God's secret communication, it makes sense that ministers who seek to do God's will seek to be strengthened in this way.

A CHRIST-CENTERED LIFE

Ministers who are Christ-centered echo the desire of John the Baptist that they may decrease in order that the Lord may increase. As ministers feel the burden of their own sinfulness, they may try to deflect praise or recognition from others. They are more apt to put the needs of others before their own, and do so graciously. In the process, they become more sensitive to issues of justice and the environment as they begin to see the world as a manifestation of God's love. As their hearts expand in response to God's hidden communication, their thinking becomes inclusive rather than exclusive. The passage in Matthew's Gospel, "Amen, I say to you, whatever you did for one of these least brothers of mine, you did for me" (Mt 25:40b) becomes particularly meaningful as they strive to see Christ in their brothers and sisters.

As God continues to beckon in ways that are increasingly unknown, the active and passive nights complement one another. By means of increased detachment and through a cloud of uncertainty, God leads those with a Christ-centered heart more deeply into the mystery of his love. As the passive night overshadows the clarity that was experienced earlier in the journey, God invites those at this stage into a deeper sense of surrender. As a black and white perspective fades into shades of gray, self-righteousness is replaced by a more pastoral disposition. Rooted in both gentleness and justice, these ministers are gradually transformed into human examples of the compassion of Christ. Depending on a minister's previous notions about the active apostolate, this change can be disconcerting and even frightening, as the Spirit leads them beyond a former certitude that was more exclusive than inclusive.

But lest fear or discouragement overcome those who feel their world has been turned upside down, John of the Cross wisely cautions them not to fear the risk of being lost as they enter uncharted territory. The saint offers the following explanation of God's action at this stage.

> God so curbs concupiscence and bridles the appetites through this dark and arid night that the soul cannot feast on any sensory delight from earthly or heavenly things and He continues the purgation in such a way that the concupiscence and the appetites are brought into subjection, reformed and mortified.[3]

At this stage, ministers are being asked to give up control so that God can guide them beyond the confines of previous comfort zones. As they continue the journey, a sense of loss is accompanied by a sense of longing for the security of times past. Since hope can be present only in the absence of that which is longed for, the absence of consolation and certainty increases the need to depend on faith to guide the way.

Paradoxically, this hidden communication of God creates an inner peace which is present even in the midst of conflict. As John of the Cross notes, "When the appetites and concupiscences are quenched, the soul dwells in spiritual solace and tranquility."[4] Similarly, St. Teresa of Avila wrote, "Be convinced that where humility is truly present, God will give a peace and conformity – even though He may never give consolations – by which one will walk with greater contentment than will others with their consolations."[5] One of the fruits of humility is the awareness of the goodness of others and an eagerness to acknowledge them. This allows humble ministers to listen and be led even as they are being called to lead.

A GRACED PERSPECTIVE

As persons become more experienced in the ways of God, they will be more inclined to measure both the quality of their prayer life and the quality of their ministry by the presence of virtue in their lives. Those in ministry move beyond personal accomplishments as a benchmark for evaluating ministry. Instead, they pay closer attention to the presence of charity in their life.

In forgetting self and placing oneself at the service of the Body of Christ, faith is put into action and hearts are purified. With the appetites less tempted by worldly pleasures and honors, ministers find the thought of returning to a former lifestyle distasteful. Higher salaries, prestige or a more carefree life no longer hold the same appeal they once did. Temptations that at one time distracted ministers from their mission no longer have the same hold over them; therefore, time is used in a more constructive and efficient manner.

Like Jesus who was led into the wilderness following His Baptism, those who seek to know and follow Jesus accept the sacrificial dimension of prayer. In short, they are better able to accept challenges and difficulties in their lives as they embrace the cross rather than resist it. In prayer, this manifests itself in the absence of consolation. In ministry, it often translates into an absence of approval from others or tangible results that feed the ego and provide personal satisfaction.

• • •

Joe, a high school religion teacher, believed that his job was all about faith. He planted seeds which he rarely saw bear fruit. He observed that most of the students viewed the course as one more class. It was required and the motivating factor for the majority seemed to be a good grade. Rarely did he witness the lessons he taught in the classroom translate into real life. And yet, he felt called to persevere. Joe devoted his life to instructing young people in the faith, challenging them to integrate faith into the world around them against what seemed to be insurmountable odds. Only on rare occasions did he receive a "thank you" from students who would come back or write to share their faith journey. Although there were times when he questioned his resolve, he could not imagine doing anything else. The peace that came in knowing that he was doing God's will was enough.

Every now and then he would see eyes light up in the classroom during a particular lesson. And while that type of reassurance felt good, it was no longer the driving force that kept him faithful. He did what he did because he held fast to the belief that the seeds he was planting today would bear fruit tomorrow. Early on in his career, grace had carried Joe beyond the disillusionment which often causes some to abandon the profession. Over time, he realized that teaching was not just a profession. It was his vocation; a vocation within his vocation as husband and father. For him, God's hidden communication was understood in the presence of an inner peace that defied logic but nevertheless sustained him. That is not to say that he was not tempted or that he never became disheartened. Joe still had to work with the grace of the moment but, in accepting that grace, he was given the courage to remain faithful to what he knew in his heart was God's will for him.

• • •

Again we turn to John of the Cross to shed light on this process.

> When the sensory appetites, gratifications and supports are quenched, the intellect is left limpid and free to understand the truth, for even though these concern spiritual things, they blind and impede the spirit. Similarly the anguish and dryness of the senses illumines and quickens the intellect…But God also, by means of this dark and dry night of contemplation, supernaturally instructs in His divine wisdom the soul that is empty and unhindered… which He did not do through former satisfactions and pleasures.[6]

As those who wait in darkness experience the void of sensual gratification, be it in prayer or in ministry, they focus more and more on the God of consolation rather than on the consolations of God. In the absence of words, they rest in His presence and there they discover the strength to be faithful.

• • •

When Joe had been tempted to give up teaching, he found the strength he needed by reflecting on the words of Jesus who warned that those who put their hand to the plow and keep looking back are not worthy of the Kingdom. In allowing the Scripture passage to seep into his heart, Joe realized that every time he questioned his call, he was rethinking his "yes" to God. By saying, "no" to his imagination, which lured him to the life he could have if he had chosen another career track, Joe experienced the peace that comes in following the will of God. But saying "no" is not a once and for all occurrence. Temptations will continue to plague those who take their call seriously, but over time their resolve to resist temptations becomes habitual and faithful obedience to that call requires less effort.

Joe found that turning to prayer more frequently gave him the strength to continue. Prayer enabled him to move beyond obstacles encountered along the way and to embrace what conventional wisdom viewed as folly. He shared with me that he was better able to appreciate his unique vocation when he tried to be faithful one moment at a time. In the end, it made him a more dedicated teacher.

• • •

Translating self-knowledge into behavioral change is a process that takes time. Like acquiring any habit, change happens only after repeated attempts and failures. In the beginning, it may be so subtle that it goes unnoticed and often is realized only in retrospect. Recall that at the Last Supper, Jesus got up from table and began to wash the feet of the disciples. But when He approached Peter, the apostle objected to Jesus washing his feet to which the Lord responded, "What I am doing you do not understand now, but you will understand later" (Jn 13:7).

The act of Jesus washing the feet of the apostles was more than an act of hospitality. It was about more than the customary cleansing of road dust from the feet of guests. Jesus was showing His followers what it meant to be a servant. Only later would they understand what He had done. In a similar manner, the process of passive purgation and God's hidden communication can only be appreciated by hearts that are humble, and then often only in retrospect. Like Peter, who finally permitted Jesus to wash his feet after he was told, "Unless I wash you, you will have no inheritance with me" (Jn 13:8), they allow God to do for them what they cannot accomplish on their own.

EVIDENCE OF GOD'S SELF-REVELATION

Despite doubt and feelings of unworthiness, ministers who believe that God is leading them are proof that God is working in their soul in ways they cannot fathom. As natural appetites are purified, some may experience God's self-communication in ways that we often refer to as "graced moments." It may happen that a Scripture passage offers insight or clarity, as was the case with Joe.

Most in ministry have experienced occasions when a prepared text or lesson gives way to a direction they had not thought about previously. Much to their surprise, the words flow with ease and listeners resonate with the message in a way the minister could not have predicted. It happens unexpectedly, surprising the speaker, leaving him or her with a sense that it was the Holy Spirit that inspired the words. Rather than feeling puffed up by pride, such graced events leave ministers feeling humbled, knowing that God has chosen to use them in ways they could not have imagined. If anything, they become more aware of their own sinfulness and their interior disposition becomes like that of the Roman centurion, who exclaimed, "Lord, I am not worthy to have you come under my roof" (Mt 8:8a).

With an increase of humility comes an increase in the theological virtues of faith, hope and love which bear witness to the efficacy of God's hidden communication during the dark night of sense. Virtues which persons struggled to acquire in the past begin to flow effortlessly as an outflow of God's presence within. Due to an awareness of God's mercy, these humble hearts are more compassionate in dealing with the failings of others and are better able to respond in charity to the demands of ministry. They continue despite criticism and misunderstanding, often against seemingly overwhelming odds. As John points out:

> Were it not for the satisfaction that God Himself sometimes infuses, it would be a wonder if the soul through its own diligence could get any sensible gratification or consolation out of its spiritual works and exercises. In this arid night solicitude for God and yearnings about serving Him increase.[7]

John continues to acknowledge that all this is the result of sheer grace. He knows from experience that aridity and deprivation of sensory satisfaction equip the soul with the courage necessary to continue the journey that leads to transformation. With the passions of joy, sorrow, hope and fear now calmed by the dark night of sense, the soul is prepared to enter the next night, which is the night of the spirit.

And yet, the fight against the senses is not over. As ministers experience periods of graced understanding, the need for vigilance continues. John explains that further temptations, which he refers to as "these loathsome spirits" are sent not to cause the downfall of those who receive them, but to prepare them for the night that is to follow. Providing somewhat of a warning, John wrote:

> The spirit so darkens the senses that it fills them with a thousand scruples and perplexities, and these seem so intricate to them that they can never be content with anything, nor can their judgment receive the support of any counsel or idea. This is one of the most burdensome goads and horrors of this night – very similar to what occurs in the spiritual night.[8]

Bereft of prior consolations, persons at this stage do well to heed the counsel of St. Teresa who advised, "The important thing is not to think much but to love much."

Although she is writing about prayer, those who experience interior conflict regarding the path on which God is leading them can profit from her advice. Her simple, straightforward approach reminds conflicted souls to position themselves at the Lord's feet. It is there that they will be strengthened by God's hidden communication.

The length and intensity of the night of sense varies from person to person. John maintains that God keeps those who are very weak in the night of sense for a long time. Some arrive at this level of purgation very late in life and some may never get there at all. According to the saint, those who are weak may experience the night for short periods interspersed with periods of relief so as not to discourage them altogether.

But those who have been purified sufficiently to have passed through the night of sense once again find themselves at a threshold. As good as this is, it is not perfect. And Jesus invited us to be perfectly united with Him; to be one with Him as He is one with the Father. This can be accomplished only through further purification in what John termed the night of spirit. According to John however, when God intends to lead the soul on, he does not plunge it into the night of spirit immediately after it has emerged from the night of sense. They are granted somewhat of a reprieve by way of preparation for what is to come. At this point, with appetites purified as well as they can be, these souls resonate with the words of John of the Cross, "My house now all stilled." Having left the way of beginners, they are about to enter what John calls the way of proficients or what is traditionally referred to as the illuminative way.

JOURNALING QUESTIONS

1. How have I experienced God's hidden communication?
2. What has been my response?
3. After all this time, do I still see myself as being center-stage?
4. How have I empowered others to build the Kingdom?
5. What roles do Eucharist, the Sacrament of Reconciliation and personal prayer play in my life?
6. How have the passions of joy, sorrow, hope and fear been stilled in my life?

CHAPTER VIII

THE ILLUMINATIVE STAGE

BRIDGE TO THE DARK NIGHT OF THE SPIRIT

The illuminative way serves as a bridge between the night of the senses and the night of the spirit. Those who are brought to this stage are considered proficient in the spiritual life. With hearts illumined by the knowledge that they are loved, they are more secure in their relationship with God. However, both John and Teresa agree that while many enter this stage, few pass beyond it.

At the beginning of her discussion of the fourth dwelling place, where most would place the illuminative way, St. Teresa writes about the "prayer of quiet" and regards it as the beginning of infused contemplation. These brief moments of absorption are short-lived and are not the result of human effort. During the experience, the will is captivated, although the faculties of imagination and memory may be wandering. Teresa describes this as a time of consolation and explains that prayer is accompanied by "spiritual delights." She uses the analogy of a well-spring, likening prayer to water that is flowing from deep within. Having experienced aridity and difficulty in prayer, prayer now becomes easy and consolations are frequent.

John of the Cross offers a similar description of prayer. "At the moment it recollects itself in the presence of God, it enters upon an act of general, loving, peaceful and tranquil knowledge, drinking wisdom and love and delight."[1] In describing what is traditionally called the illuminative stage, he wrote:

> In this new state, as one liberated from a cramped prison cell, [the soul] goes about the things of God with much more freedom and satisfaction of spirit and with more abundant spiritual delight than it did in the beginning before entering the night of sense. Its imagination and faculties are no longer bound to discursive meditation and spiritual solicitude as was their custom. The soul readily finds in its spirit, without the work of meditation, a very serene, loving contemplation and spiritual delight.[2]

Freed from the bondage of disordered appetites, the serenity that accompanies contemplation can be likened to the relaxed atmosphere that is felt between two people who are falling in love. They no longer feel compelled to expend time and energy looking for ways to entertain or be entertained. Having come to the awareness that sharing one another's company is the best use of their time together, they are content.

As for ministers: accomplishments that they may have viewed as proof of their love for God in the past now become less important than the One who called them. For those who long for union with God, prayer is a way to be with God who loves them. And ministry is a way to repay love with love. As those in the illuminative stage continue to experience the warmth of God's presence within, prayer becomes more and more the vehicle through which they seek God and through which God affirms them. In response to the God who loved them first, ministers likewise commit themselves to the task at hand with a fervor that is rooted in their relationship with God.

Both Sts. Teresa and John warn against the perception that the illuminative stage is an ongoing state of spiritual delight. Teresa wrote that she would be suspicious of anyone who claimed to be in a habitual state of absorption. Although both saints were writing specifically about prayer, their insights can also be applied to ministers who have reached this stage of commitment. For having reached this stage, ministers, too, have experienced infused contemplation, even though they may not call it by that name.

With hearts increasingly more focused on God as the reason for their labor, these ministers respond to others in a more joyful manner. They go about their work with a lightness of heart characteristic of lovers. With little effort on their part, heartfelt praise and gratitude resound deep within even while exercising the most mundane tasks. Their love and fervor serve as a backdrop that puts a song in their heart and a spring in their step. These ministers discover a new joy in tasks they had previously found wearisome. God seems to beckon to them in both subtle and profound ways. A deeper awareness of God's presence allows them to recognize the humanity of Christ in the people they serve and ordinary tasks are valued as holy.

Since those who have been brought to the illuminative way have acquired greater self-discipline and have reordered their priorities according to God's law of love, sensory gratification that flows from their ministry no longer poses as grave a threat as it did in the night of sense. And yet, temptations must still be overcome, as committing sin still remains a possibility. As John and Teresa teach, the spirit – that deepest part of the human person – has yet to be purified. And as a result, ongoing vigilance is essential. John cautions that during the illuminative stage, "proficients are easily charmed and beguiled." [3] His advice is to reject any extraordinary experiences of God's presence and depend solely on faith. Some criticize his stern approach, but the saint holds firm that the devil is very active at this stage, trying to entice those who experience spiritual phenomena to see themselves as special or believe themselves to be more advanced than they actually are.

The same temptations accost those who are in ministry. It may stem from the joy and success they experience, which they attribute to God, but, in fact, they believe

God has blessed them with spiritual favors because of their love for him. Pride once again becomes their greatest enemy, and so what began as a favor can actually lead to sin. Any thinking that sets a person apart is dangerous and becomes a stumbling block on the road to Christian perfection. St. Paul's advice to the Philippians – "Do nothing out of selfishness or vainglory; rather, humbly regard others as more important than yourselves, each looking out not for his own interest, but [also] everyone for those of others" (Phil 2:3-4) – is a helpful reminder for those tempted to claim as their own what God is accomplishing through them. On this same subject, Teresa wrote, "The first sign for seeing whether or not you have humility is that you think you deserve these favors and spiritual delights from the Lord or that you will receive them in your lifetime."[4]

Recall that Jesus reminded us not to put new wine into old wine skins. As the wine ferments, it will cause old skins that have shrunk to burst. In a similar manner, fruits of a God-centered relationship cannot be contained by hearts shrunken by self-love. Unless persons set aside old ways of approaching God, motivated by sensory pleasure, their hearts will not be able to contain the new wine of Christ's love. As God illumines hearts, He re-creates them in His image and, in turn, they become docile and more willing to serve others.

POVERTY OF SPIRIT

Throughout the ages, God has chosen the lowest and most unlikely people to be his apostles and prophets. In *Ministries: Sharing God's Gifts*, Father James Dunning suggests that those who enter ministry must set aside criteria based on a business model that chooses the most qualified candidates for employment. He goes on to say that while matching talents and gifts is one consideration, there is another question that needs to be asked:

> Is that man weak enough to be a priest; is this woman fragile enough to be a servant-healer? Is this person vulnerable enough so that he/she cannot banish suffering from life, so that she feels what it is to be an ordinary woman who shares the human journey and stumbles and bumbles along the path that we all share? Does he know fear, loneliness, failure and self-doubt, and still gather to offer Eucharist, to give thanks to the God who fills us precisely where we are empty?[5]

Humility must be the underlying virtue for ministers just as Teresa and John insisted for those who wish to advance along the path to union through prayer. Ministers must move away from the model of the corporate ladder where achievement and productivity serve as criteria for valuing a person's worth. In looking for a model for ministers, we need look no further than Jesus of Nazareth, the Incarnate Son of God.

Writing about the radical step that God took in becoming man, Johannes Baptist Metz, author of the spiritual classic *Poverty of Spirit* wrote "to become man means to become poor, to have nothing which one might brag about before God."[6] Jesus' becoming human was not an empty show. Jesus, "though he was in the form of God did not regard equality with God something to be grasped. Rather, he emptied himself" (Phil 2:6-7). Jesus' sole desire was to do the will of His Father in all things, even if it meant dying a cruel and merciless death. He consistently chose the most unlikely way. Beginning with His being born into poverty to being stripped and hung upon the cross, every word, every action of Jesus was a lesson in self-emptying. But, His poverty was not limited to physical poverty. Metz captured the magnitude of Jesus' interior poverty, not to be confused with weakness, in writing about the temptations during His forty days in the desert.

> Satan's temptation calls upon Jesus to remain strong like God, to stand within a protecting circle of angels, to hang onto his divinity. He urges Jesus not to plunge into the loneliness and futility that is a real part of human existence. He urges him to flee from the desert (the prototype of man's abject poverty), to sneak away from our miserable lot that cries out to heaven. For hunger becomes hunger only when it can never be allayed; desire becomes a human desire only when it can remain unfulfilled. Jesus' "no" to Satan is His "yes" to our poverty.[7]

Satan promised Jesus that which gratified the senses: bread, power and esteem, but Jesus saw through his charade. Metz noted that had Jesus succumbed to Satan's wiles, the Incarnation would have lost its meaning, for Jesus would have been man in name only. The God-man was subject to the kind of darkness that meant He, too, had to journey in faith like every other believer. His journey led him to Calvary. Jesus chose the cross not because He wanted to suffer but because He understood that death will always precede life. In choosing the cross, Jesus chose what Metz called the "sacrament of poverty of spirit."[8]

There is nothing holy about poverty. But when we surrender all to God for the sake of God's Kingdom, then poverty becomes the means of self-emptying and the ultimate surrender. Like Jesus, all who desire to do the will of the Father must embrace their own poverty. When they do, they are illumined about the need for deeper and more profound purgation, which takes place in the night of the spirit.

Those whom God brings to this night are blessed. But all who enter this night of the spirit, whether they view their primary calling as the active apostolate or the contemplative life, will encounter the same question: Am I willing to be stripped of everything like Jesus, that weak and vulnerable man who hung on the cross?

PURGATION CONTINUES

Souls who have reached the illuminative way have tasted the sweet communications of the spirit. They have discovered there is more to living in relationship with God than they once knew. But since their longing for God has been gratified with spiritual delights, some wrongly believe they will remain this way indefinitely. But, if God chooses to bring persons into the way of the perfect, darkness will once again descend. The very ones who only a short time ago felt secure in God's love find themselves not on the marriage bed but on the cross. In the fullness of His humanity, Jesus cried out, "My God, my God, why have you forsaken me?" (Mk 15:34) And, like Him, those who continue on the path toward union will enter the night of the spirit.

John offers the following explanation as to why those who wish to be perfect must endure further purgation:

> The real purgation of the senses begins with the spirit. Hence the night of the senses we explained should be called a certain reformation and bridling of the appetite rather than a purgation. The reason is that all the imperfections and disorders of the sensory part are rooted in the spirit and from it receive its strength. All good and evil habits reside in the spirit and until these habits are purged, the senses cannot be completely purified of their rebellions and vices.[9]

Both John and Teresa caution that the night of spirit is more intense than anything encountered thus far. This is not meant to frighten or discourage those whom God brings to this level of purgation, but to prepare them for the purification that lies ahead. Always the realists, they remind those who think they have experienced death on the cross that Calvary is still a long way off. Their warnings serve as a reality check for proficients who naively mistake fleeting encounters with God through infused contemplation with the spiritual marriage.

JOURNALING QUESTIONS

1. How have I experienced prayer as a restorative power in my life?
2. In what way have I tried to put new wine into old wine skins?
3. What were the consequences?
4. When I said "yes" to ministry, did I say "yes" to the cross?
5. When the storm clouds in ministry gather, do I run for cover, or do I place myself at the foot of the cross with my eyes on Jesus?

Part III
The Night of the Spirit

CHAPTER IX

DYING TO THE SENSES

AN ONGOING PURIFICATION

The night of the spirit has the same three-fold purpose as the night of the senses: mortification of the senses, journeying in faith and God's hidden communication. However, in referring to the night of the spirit, the phrase "dying to the senses" rather than "mortification of the senses" is more fitting, because it more accurately describes the negation of sensory dependency that is present there. John of the Cross offers a clear explanation of the difference between the night of the senses and the night of the spirit. "The difference between the two purgations is like the difference between pulling up roots and cutting off a branch, or rubbing out a fresh stain or an old, deeply embedded one."[1]

He explains that habitual affections and imperfections that remain rooted in the spirit are further purified and put to rest during this night. "The spirit must be illumined, clarified and recollected by means of the hardships and conflicts of this night."[2] The saint warned those who are serious about finding union with God that the night of spirit is more intense than anything they had experienced previously.

This chapter will explore how this occurs and how dying to the senses pertains to ministers who are brought to the night of spirit. The next two chapters will address ways that ministers may experience journeying in faith and God's hidden communication during this night. A suitable analogy for the more advanced stages of the spiritual life may be found in Luke's Gospel in the account foretelling of the birth of John the Baptist. Zechariah's experience offers an illustration of God's purifying action in the soul within the context of life situations.

> In the days of Herod, King of Judea, there was a priest named Zechariah of the priestly division of Abijah; his wife was from the daughters of Aaron, and her name was Elizabeth. Both were righteous in the eyes of god, observing all the commandments and ordinances of the Lord blamelessly. But they had no child, because Elizabeth was barren and both were advanced in years. (Lk 1:5-7).

Since children were regarded as a sign of God's blessing, being childless was a hardship for devout Jews such as Zechariah and Elizabeth. Yet in the seeming absence of divine favor, the couple remained steadfast in their faith in the Lord. It is not unusual for those who are proficient in the spiritual life to equate blessings, experiences of consolation and God's felt presence as a sign of God's approval. However, if these spiritual seekers are to advance from proficient to perfect, they must set aside such notions. To assist them in this process, God brings persons at this stage into the passive night of spirit, since they are unable to accomplish this on their own. Although this passive night is internal in nature, it is brought about through external circumstances over which persons have no control.

And so it happens that just when proficients feel secure in their approach to prayer and their relationship with God, both change. Images and forms of prayer to which they had grown accustomed are no longer helpful, and without warning God seems as illusive and distant as he once seemed near. As a way to understand this phenomenon, consider once again Zechariah, who remained faithful to his priestly duties despite the fact that the couple had not been blessed with children.

> Once when he was serving as priest in his division's turn before God, according to the practice of the priestly service, he was chosen by lot to enter the sanctuary of the Lord to burn incense. Then, when the whole assembly of people was praying outside at the hour of the incense offering, the angle of the Lord appeared to him, standing at the right of the altar of incense. Zechariah was troubled by what he saw, and fear came upon him. But the angel said to him, 'Do not be afraid, Zechariah, because your prayer has been heard. Your wife Elizabeth will bear you a son, and you shall name him John. And you will have joy and gladness, and many will rejoice at his birth, for he will be great in the sight of [the] Lord.' (Lk 1:8-14)

Once God drew Zechariah beyond his comfort zone, he was understandably frightened. Scripture tells us that he responded with doubt and asked, "How shall I know this? For I am an old man, and my wife is advanced in years" (Lk 1:18). In questioning the angel's message, Zechariah trusted the known over the unknown, chose reason over faith and human wisdom over the wisdom of God. Zechariah's interior struggle, manifested by his doubting the angel, provides a window of understanding into an all-too-human response. In the presence of the unknown, the natural inclination is to resist, to seek a logical explanation or to ignore the unfamiliar as a way to hold on to what we believe is factual. Zechariah's experience was an external encounter with an angel of the Lord, which is not to be confused with infused prayer or contemplation. However, as spiritual seekers are led into a deeper and purer experience of God, the senses are by-passed and God's presence is no longer experienced through the intellect. Even as proficients long to spend time alone with God, they are victims of doubt and uncertainty in the uncharted waters of contemplative prayer, proof that further purification is required as was the case with Zechariah.

> And the angel replied, I am Gabriel, who stand before God. I was sent to speak to you and to announce to you this good news. But now you will be speechless and unable to talk until the days these things take place, because you did not believe my words, which will be fulfilled at their proper time. (Lk 1:19-20)

Zechariah doubted the angel's words and he became mute. Rather than punishment, it was an invitation for him to enter more deeply into the ways of God. Not being able to speak until his son was born was obviously a source of physical and emotional suffering for Zechariah, but there was also an interior and more spiritual suffering taking place. This spiritual anguish contributed to the purification of Zechariah's will during those months of silence.

After Elizabeth gave birth and announced the baby's name would be John, even though no family member had the name John, Zechariah readily agreed. He complied with the angel's instruction without hesitation, which indicates that his will had been reconciled with the will of God. An interior transformation had taken place during those months of silence. When Zechariah wrote, "[h]e will be called John" (Lk 1:60), Scripture records that he was able to speak immediately. The loosening of his tongue is analogous to the interior freedom experienced by those who, by means of the night of the spirit, are detached from sensory gratification at its root level.

A similar comparison can be drawn with those in ministry who have acquired a degree of proficiency. Knowledge plus experience translates into expending less energy to accomplish tasks that were previously labor- intensive. These ministers now carry out their duties with confidence and ease, confident that God is blessing their efforts. Secure in a more relaxed approach to ministry, they remain committed to their apostolate; that is, until life takes an unexpected turn and things become unpredictable.

Life happens and in the process misfortunes and setbacks of all types occur. Some regard these as punishments, but a more faith-filled perspective invites us to view them as grace-filled moments. Experiences that draw us beyond a level of comfort that is no longer challenging strip away former misconceptions. When embraced, these experiences, painful though they may be, destroy obstacles deeply embedded in the human psyche. This interior suffering, which is part of the continued purgative process, is what John of the Cross would consider dying to the senses according to the night of spirit. Like Jesus who journeyed to Jerusalem even though He knew it would mean His death, those who wish to be perfect must sever the bonds that keep them from following Christ to Calvary, for there is no other way to die to self.

FREEDOM THROUGH SURRENDER

John of the Cross maintained that it matters little whether we are tethered by a rope or a string. The attachment keeps us from soaring. As persons advance in the way of prayer, the attachments are less easy to recognize. They are deeply engrained and can often be traced back to experiences that played a role during the formative years of human development. Consequently, they often reside on an unconscious level and are revealed only during a crisis. The resistance is most often rooted in fear. When life situations take us beyond our comfort zone, the natural pull is to return to what is familiar. Therefore, the work of the dark night is to free us from old ways of making meaning of life's events in order to be open to the will of God.

Securities that we once relied on are snatched away. We have nothing to cling to. Those in this stage of the dark night often seek reassurance in the story of Job as they are stripped of previous attachments such as human respect or the ability to take charge or be in control of their lives. But crises purify those whom God brings into this night of spirit. The characteristic that sets them apart from others who resist the purgation is the peace that accompanies the pain. The more they abandon themselves to God during moments of crisis, the greater their serenity.

• • •

During a parish retreat, Ray shared that as a teacher he had been very judgmental about the parents of some his teenage students. When students behaved disrespectfully, were unprepared for class or got into trouble outside of school, he was the first to lay the blame at the feet of their parents. But when his own daughter got into trouble and was missing for a week, he felt utterly helpless. For the first time, Ray understood what some of the parents of his students had been going through. After his daughter returned home and the family went through extensive counseling, their relationship improved and so did the way Ray viewed his students and their parents. He shared that although the experience had been very painful, it helped him realize how self-righteous he had been. When Ray no longer felt he was in control, he abandoned himself to God. Not only did the experience deepen his relationship with God, but it helped him to be more sensitive when working with struggling students and their parents.

• • •

Often the tendency to be judgmental or self-righteous can be traced to childhood. Thomas Merton defined the false self as a product of collective expectations and criticisms of others. They become embedded, often on an unconscious level, but for the true self to emerge the old self must be stripped away. This is the purgative work that is accomplished in the night of spirit. When the false self is uprooted, lay ministers are free to be transformed into servants that are centered in God. The more the false self is stripped away, the more persons discover their true identity in God. As they are united with the sufferings of Christ, they become one with the Father.

Mother Teresa of Calcutta referred to herself as a pencil in God's hand. It is an appropriate image for lay ministers who strive to give up control so that God can use them in ways they could not have imagined. It also serves as a reminder that every good work accomplished, every success enjoyed, is the result of God's grace. When we admire a masterpiece, we credit the artist, not the brush. Similarly, when those in the active apostolate are centered in God, they attribute the fruits of their labor to the divine artist. They grow into this deeper appreciation over time by trusting the darkness.

• • •

Rita, a lay minister at a large parish, confided that she felt rejected when she was passed over for a job she had applied for with the diocese. She had been confident that she would be named to the position, but when a deacon was hired for the position, she was both hurt and angry. She felt her years of service had been underappreciated and was tempted to walk away not only from ecclesial ministry but from the Church. No matter how much she prayed, the darkness became more intense.

Rita decided to take a week-long retreat to help her discern what to do. While on retreat, a journaling exercise revealed old wounds that were rooted in feelings of rejection. As she sat alone in the chapel one evening, her life seemed to play before her like a movie. All the hurts, both past and present, were as real as they were when she experienced them, particularly the woundedness that was rooted by her father walking out on the family when she was a child. The feeling of being unloved that plagued her as a child had come back. Anger had been her only defense, but once the mask of the false self was stripped away, she no longer needed the promotion to prove that she was loved. She felt God's healing love in the darkness of her midnight hour and was able to surrender to God's grace.

• • •

Such insights act like microscopes that reveal wounds and disordered attachments hidden deep within the human psyche. Once they are exposed, we are faced with a decision. We can surrender to God who is inviting us to deeper trust by dying to self, or we can remain in our comfort zone. John of the Cross assured us that when we go forth "fired with love's urgent longings," we depart from a less perfect way of loving. The departure is a deliberate and often a difficult choice. But once freed from the captivity of the senses, we are able to unite our will with the will of God. And all is the result of grace. The saint shared his interior experience as God led him from the darkness of self-protection into the light of faith.

> This was great happiness and a sheer grace for me, because through annihilation and calming of my faculties, passions, appetites, and affections, by which my experience and satisfaction in God were base, I went out from my human operation and way of acting to God's operation and way of acting. That is: My intellect departed from itself, changing from human and natural to divine. For united with God through this purgation, it no longer understands by means of its natural vigor

> and light, but by means of the divine wisdom to which it was united. And my will departed from itself and became divine. United with the divine love, it no longer loves in a lowly manner, with its natural strength, but with the strength and purity of the Holy Spirit; and thus the will does not operate humanly in relation to God.[3]

As lay ministers journey through the night of spirit, they discover that their love for God is being purified. Gradually dying to the senses provides the means by which they are purged of all that prevents their will from being one with the will of God as it unfolds within the context of life.

PEAKS AND VALLEYS

The spiritual masters agree that the higher the peak, the deeper the valley as the soul continues the journey toward union with God. It seems that just when spiritual seekers believe they are making progress, they are thrown into a situation that causes them to question much of what they had come to accept and even rely on, particularly in regard to experiences of consolation in prayer.

John cautions these persons to set aside prayer experiences that delight the senses or tempt them to think they are special or more advanced than others. He warns them that Satan and human weakness can masquerade as experiences of God and so he urges those committed to contemplative prayer to pay no attention to exceptional experiences. Recounting them to a wise spiritual guide is important, but then the saint advises that they should be set aside as though they never happened. He insists that if the experiences are from God, the grace has already been received and unless thinking about it increases one's love for God, they no longer serve a purpose. According to the saint, those who cling to them as a source of comfort during times of difficulty are actually impeding the journey to union.

I find parallels to this phenomenon in ministry. Over the years, I have been privileged to be a spiritual director for a number of lay ministers, both professionals and volunteers. I have found that there is a tendency, among some, to regard their ministry as being more spiritual than other types of work, but this type of thinking is a pitfall. We have no way of knowing how or why God chooses people to do his work. The human tendency to judge invites error. I sometimes suggest that ministers reflect on the Gospel account of the widow's mite when this temptation becomes an obstacle. The example of the widow who gave a meager amount, but at great sacrifice, can help ministers remain humble when they feel they are giving more than some and are therefore more pleasing to God.

I have found many ministers come to this awareness through what John would regard as a dark night experience. One of the most humbling and purgative experiences that I have observed comes not through work but ministers' personal lives.

It sometimes happens that those who have devoted their lives to God experience discord with spouses or family members. The initial reaction is sorrow and embarrassment. They may fear they will be judged by others as hypocrites. How can they preach faith and family values to others when their own life seems to be falling apart? But the reality is that ministers and their families are not immune from human frailty and societal pressures.

• • •

When Jane's husband left her for another woman, she was devastated. How could God allow this to happen after she gave her all to his Church? Jim's daughter ran away from home and became pregnant at sixteen and Terry's son was arrested for selling drugs. Obviously, God did not cause these situations. Life is complicated and we can never fully understand why people do what they do. Yet, as painful as such experiences are – and most of them are beyond the control of the lay minister – they provide an opportunity to be purified in ways people would never seek actively.

• • •

If ministers wish to follow Christ, then they, too, must learn to embrace betrayal, criticism and rejection. When it comes through a family member or a close friend, it leaves them exposed and vulnerable. They may not be able to change the behavior of those who disappoint, but those who wish to be one with God must love unconditionally and forgive as Jesus forgave. Rather than dwell on the pain and discord, they need to be encouraged to remain faithful and love those who disappoint them or are a source of grief. It is also a lesson in letting go of the notion of entitlement, subtle though it may be. The more the hands of those who serve remain empty, the sooner they come to terms with personal limitations and rely on God for strength, particularly when it seems God is absent. John of the Cross discusses this deep and painful purgation:

> When this purgative contemplation oppresses a person, he feels very vividly indeed like the shadow of death, the sighs of death, and the sorrows of hell, all of which reflect the feeling of God's absence, of being chastised and rejected by Him, and of being untrustworthy of Him, as well as the object of His anger. The soul experiences all this and even more, for now it seems the affliction will last forever. A person also feels forsaken and despised by creatures, particularly by his friends.[4]

So great is the suffering that it assails those in the night of spirit from within and from the outside. Subjected to abandonment by friends or family, they experience an inner turmoil that leads them to believe they are spiritually doomed. And the judgments of those who now see them in a less than favorable light only add to the feeling that they are among the most despicable and will share no place in the Kingdom of God. Their interior posture resembles that of the good thief who, while dying, realized that he deserved nothing more. At the same time, he had only praise for Jesus who hung on the cross beside him.

Only a humble minister can call others to a Godly life, while owning their own sinfulness. Believing others are justified in their judgments, they become increasingly humble and open to the will of God. In the midst of their pain, their efforts become even more effective. As they unite their life with Jesus as suffering servant, they may never know how their decision to love, despite suffering and heartache, serves as a source of inspiration to others. Indeed, their humility may cause the self-righteous to become more introspective or offer hope to those who equate having a relationship with God as being entitled to having a problem-free life. The sense of entitlement or any expectation of being rewarded is extinguished during the night of the spirit as ministers are stripped of the remnants of all that stands between them and God.

This process cannot be rushed. Purification takes place within the context of dying and rising, in remaining faithful when human instinct wishes to run away and hide. As hearts are purified and vain thoughts and aspirations are annihilated, hearts are emptied so that God can fill them. The experience is not unlike John's description of the darkness of contemplation:

> The soul not only suffers the void and suspension of these natural supports and apprehensions, which is a terrible anguish (like hanging in midair unable to breathe) but it is also purged by this contemplation. As fire consumes the tarnish and rust of metal, this contemplation annihilates, empties and consumes all the affections and imperfect habits the soul contracted throughout its life.[5]

What husband or wife has not felt as though the breath was sucked from their very being when their spouse died or asked for a divorce? And what parent does not feel as if their heart were torn from them when a child follows a path that leads to self-destruction? Such experiences invite those who wish to be perfect to die to their will and seek the will of God amid the sufferings of life. In the process, faith is strengthened and hearts are purified on the level of spirit. Those who are led along this path emerge with greater wisdom and a deep and abiding sense of humility. Like Job who at last was free to praise God in circumstances that were both good and bad, ministers who embrace the cross will experience the wisdom of God on a deep and profound level. Hope in God's mercy is the only recourse for those who pass through this night, and peace and tranquility carry them in ways that surprise all whom they encounter.

Those who seek to rid themselves of the string that still binds them to the false self must open themselves to Jesus, who embraced the whole world from the cross. In the midst of excruciating pain, the work of the night of spirit is being accomplished. Those who embrace it journey deeper into the heart of God. Ministers who hang on the cross with Jesus mirror the humility and profound love of God. Their lives become a living witness of the mandate to preach the Gospel through actions as well as words.

JOURNALING QUESTIONS

1. When I consider the possibility of entering the night of spirit, what is my reaction?
2. Have I been purified by way of the night of spirit?
3. How has the passive night of spirit humbled me?
4. What have I learned from the experience?
5. How has it affected my work in the ministry?
6. How has the experience impacted my relationship with God?

CHAPTER X
JOURNEYING IN FAITH

THE FELT ABSENCE OF GOD

For the sake of clarity, I have discussed dying to the senses, journeying in faith and God's hidden communication in separate chapters. However, they are not exclusive of each other. In fact, the three are so closely related that at times their relationship seems to be one of cause and effect.

Dark night experiences are played out in the course of life within the context of disappointments and crises. They may take the form of unrequited love, family discord, illness, financial loss, or the death of a loved one, to name a few. But regardless of whether darkness enters our life like a grey fog that slowly overtakes us, appears like a starless night that is filled with doubts and desolation, or descends on us with a force that feels like a full blown state of depression, we are called to believe that God is at work, purifying and strengthening the soul in the midst of utter darkness. Amid suffering and what feels like an absence of God, those who strive to unite their will with the will of God continue the journey in faith, for it can be no other way. Were God to rescue those who are suffering prematurely, faith would be irrelevant. And it is faith that leads us to the inner sanctum of the soul where God dwells.

To journey in faith means believing in an illusive God whose touch is invisible, because to give in to despair would be inconceivable. It means believing that we are being healed during God's seeming absence more than during times of his felt presence. As the voice of God grows increasingly more obscure, the last vestiges of the false self fade away and, in the process, transformation gives birth to the true self. But the only way to recognize God's secret communication is to spend time alone with the Alone. It makes little difference whether we begin the journey on the path of contemplative prayer or by means of the active apostolate. Unless we surrender to the darkness that purifies and strengthens faith, we will make little progress on either.

Journals and letters written by Mother Teresa of Calcutta reveal a soul that was plagued with inner darkness for fifty years. At times interior doubt caused her to question the existence of God and yet she surrendered to what she believed was God's will for her. She complained to her spiritual directors that her heart felt as cold as stone. No one who observed her suspected the interior suffering that was taking place. Consequently, her journals offer much-needed insight about how those who long for God experience and respond to such crises of faith. As Mother Teresa went about serving the poor and calling others to do the same, her joyful presence concealed the suffering that she experienced in the depths of her soul. The purity of her love and faith would not allow her the luxury of complaining or engaging in self-pity. When persons no longer feel the reassurance of God's presence or approval but continue the journey, they walk by faith.

• • •

My friend Julie was one of these people. I first encountered Julie at daily Mass. I had just been hired as the parish Minister of Christian Formation and I was looking for volunteers for the RCIA team. I was impressed by Julie's obvious love for the Eucharist and when I asked her to serve on the team, she agreed. It did not take long for me to realize that there was something special about Julie. She was one of those people who never knew a stranger. She reached out to everyone. She was also a devoted wife and mother and managed the books for her husband's business. But within the context of a very busy life, Julie was being drawn to God in a deep and profound way. She frequently shared with me her love for God.

Eventually Julie decided to get a degree in teaching and so she juggled school with all her other duties. Still, she continued to have a smile and kind word for everyone. When it became public knowledge that her husband was having an affair, her faith in God carried her through an extremely hurtful situation. About that time Julie was hired to oversee the religious education program at the parish.

Eventually, she and her husband divorced, and just as Julie's life seemed to stabilize, tragedy struck again. This time it was in the form of a rare but rapidly growing type of cancer. Within a year Julie had died. There was standing room only in the large parish church at her Mass of the Resurrection. The bishop and priests from the area gathered together to celebrate Julie's life, but one of the most striking testimonies to Julie's faith and her relationship with God appeared in a letter to the editor in the daily newspaper. The letter, written by a hospice worker who knew Julie for only a short time, revealed the profound impact that Julie had had on her life. It led her to write the following:

> *On January 18, while some were celebrating the life of one great human being, others were mourning the loss of another. Julie Catherine Owens recently lost the year-long battle she had fought with such nobility and grace.*
>
> *When I first heard about her cancer, it became clear to me then that she was a precious gift we had all been blessed with. Enough time has not passed for our pain to disappear, for our hearts to mend, or for the tears to stop flowing, but it would only take a moment to reflect upon Julie's life to realize what an influence she was on all of us.*
>
> *She had a caring tone that made you feel as if you were her best friend. She had a*

pair of sparkling blue eyes that stared straight down to the depths of your soul. A smile that would tug at your heart and a laugh you could never forget.

As evidenced by the hundreds of people who came to tell her good-bye, she was so much to so many. What gave her the most joy was motherhood. Her two precious children have been hit the hardest. Fortunately, she had been preparing them for something of this magnitude since the day they were born.

I know I owe it to Julie to be a little more compassionate, and a little less judgmental, to give a little more to the less fortunate, to smile a whole lot more, to make children feel they are special and to do simple acts of kindness that can make our world a better place. Like it was when Julie was in it.

* (Permission has been granted by the family of Julie Catherine Owens to share her story and to identify her by name in this book).

Julie was one of those blessed souls who came to realize that everything in life is a gift. Rather than curse the darkness, she became a lantern that reflected God's light for all to see. Julie was not one to wear her faith on her sleeve. Humility would not allow such grandstanding. But in the midst of her struggle she discovered the grace hidden in the heartache of the moment. When a person's faith is present on such a deep level, it touches all who encounter it.

The tribute to Julie was not about the things she did, although her accomplishments were numerous. It was a tribute to the person she had become. And that is the sign of transformation. Those who allow God to transform them allow God's light to shine through. They are transparent. Like stained glass windows, God's light radiates from the center of their being and they bring beauty and a sense of wonder to those who are blessed to know them. Julie will always be proof that the laity are called to a deep and profoundly intimate relationship with God, which John of the Cross refers to as the spiritual marriage. Those who knew her could not doubt that Julie's will had become one with the will of God.

SUFFERING MADE HOLY

The road to spiritual maturity often runs contrary to human nature. Spiritual maturity is acquired over time and during the course of severe trials. Yet it is not the suffering that heals and transforms, but the faith of those who are afflicted which enables them to embrace the cross. According to Thomas Merton, it is the consecration of suffering, not the endurance of it, which leads to holiness.

Without consecration, suffering places us at risk. The tendency for suffering to lead to bitterness or despondency is all too real. But when suffering is placed on the altar and offered to God in thanksgiving for what God can do through suffering, it is made holy. Then, like bread and wine that are transformed during the Eucharist, hearts are transformed into the image of Christ. When pain and uncertainty, doubt and darkness are surrendered to a transcendent good, the offering is united with the agony of Jesus on Calvary. This union does not banish suffering from life. The lives of the saints are a testimony to this truth. Despite thoughts and feelings that tempt them to abandon hope, they cling to a level of faith that defies logic. Having been plunged into darkness, faith becomes their guide and enkindles the fire that lights the way to union with God.

John of the Cross is a classic example of this. Many believe that the nine months of imprisonment in Toledo was his night of the spirit. When he emerged, the profound love that filled his soul found a natural outlet in poetry and prose, which has inspired souls through the centuries. Despite his weakened health, the Carmelite friar continued to serve God through his writings, his preaching, spiritual direction, and administrative ministry in the Teresian Carmelite reform. The superiors who had banished him to a remote place in Andalusia toward the end of his life could not extinguish the flame that faith had enkindled in his heart.

John was gifted with tremendous insight regarding the spiritual journey. But not everyone who experiences union is gifted in this way. From the writings of Mother Teresa, it seems that she became aware of her deep union with God only after a spiritual director told her that her continual thirst for God was a sign of union with Jesus, who proclaimed his thirst from the cross. During one of her darkest moments, Jesus' thirst for souls gave Mother Teresa a new appreciation for her unrequited thirst for the salvation of souls.

After many years of darkness, this became a great source of consolation for her, but it took another person to point it out to her. The knowledge that her suffering was united with Jesus was comfort enough for her. Consequently, she never sought to be relieved of the darkness. In surrendering her will to God in the midst of darkness, she used her suffering as a way to bring souls to Jesus.

The lives of the saints reveal both similarities and differences. Their lives illustrate how God leads people according to the unique gifts and circumstances of their lives, which testifies to the intimacy of divine love. There are no carbon copies, only patterns that serve as blueprints to assist each person as they are led along their particular path to union with God. It bears out Jesus' reassurance that even the hairs of our head are numbered by our Father in heaven.

SURRENDERING TO THE DARKNESS

When discussing journeying through the night of the senses, I referred to the importance of trusting the darkness. Trust conveys the understanding that there is a light at the end of the tunnel; that those who remain faithful will be rewarded, even though it may not be in the way they once imagined. However, for those who journey in faith according to the night of spirit, there is no such understanding. In prayer, the memory and intellect are kept in darkness. The darkness is so intense that to see beyond it is impossible. Only a giant crevasse seems to lie ahead. With the memory and intellect surrounded by darkness, a high level of resolve is required for persons to believe when all seems hopeless. This interior darkness only adds to the soul's turmoil as external trials assail those so afflicted. John of the Cross explains what makes the night of the spirit so treacherous.

> The afflictions and straits of the will are also immense. Sometimes these afflictions pierce the soul when it suddenly remembers the evils in which itself is immersed, and it becomes uncertain of any remedy. To this pain is added the remembrance of past prosperity, because usually persons who enter this night have previously had many consolations in God and rendered him many services. They are now sorrowing in knowing that they are far from such good and can no longer enjoy it.[1]

This darkness mirrors the desolation that led Jesus to cry out "My God, my God, why have you forsaken me?" (Mk 15:34). So dark was his intellect that it seemed even his Father had abandoned him. Jesus could not see beyond the night in regard to his own well-being. And yet he was able to ask forgiveness for those who persecuted him: "Father, forgive them, they do not know what they do." (Lk 23:34) Selflessly, he responded to the good thief's plea: "Amen, I say to you, today you will be with me in paradise." (Lk 23:43)

In the presence of absolute darkness and contrary to the dictates of reason, Jesus surrendered to the belief that His dying was the will of His Father. "Jesus cried out in a loud voice, 'Father, into your hands I commend my spirit.'" (Lk 23:46)

Jesus' final act was an act of surrender to the Father, an act that seemed to defy logic and conventional wisdom. On the cross, Jesus experienced the ultimate transcendent experience, which confirmed that death must precede life. This is not a passive disposition, for to embrace death is the ultimate surrender and requires not only trust, but enormous courage. Those who seek union with the will of God are called to this same surrender. When at last persons are no longer prisoners of intentional sin, they offer their suffering in union with Jesus for their ongoing purification and salvation of others.

Anyone who attended Catholic school in the fifties grew up hearing the phrase "offer it up." It was the standard response to complaints. But it was only as an adult that I came to appreciate the efficacy of that practice. It was not meant to encourage a fatalistic mindset but to empower those who suffer. It enables those who are on the cross with Jesus to turn suffering into a life-giving reality. It means journeying in faith when all seems lost.

THE PURE OF HEART

One of the temptations in the illuminative stage is for those who receive consolations to consider themselves special because of the favors bestowed on them. But for those immensed in the night of spirit, looking back on those consolations becomes a deep source of shame and interior pain. Persons so affected believe they deserve only the wrath of God and struggle to hold onto the belief that God could actually love them. At times this seems inconceivable, as the person's faith and resolve are threatened at every turn. The temptation to despair comes in the midst of interior and external trials. Feeling that all is lost, persons at this stage often feel that they have been misled. Attacks against faith leave the soul in a state of despair, causing it to think that God that does not exist.

During such time, repeated acts of faith and the words, "my Jesus, mercy" are never far from the lips or hearts of those experiencing this crisis. The lamentations of the psalms become particularly meaningful as a source of calm amid the interior storms that tear at the fabric of faith. During this crisis, previous supports seem to be withheld, which led John of the Cross to warn: "Added to this, because of the solitude and desolation this night causes, is the fact that a person in this state finds neither consolation nor support in any doctrine or spiritual director."[2]

With every support pulled out from under them, these souls experience tremendous isolation and loneliness. Both Teresa and John warn that even spiritual directors who had at one time been supportive now seem not to understand what the person is experiencing and this only increases the pain, for they cannot discount what is said to them. Believing they are spiritually destitute, persons in this dark night of spirit may have difficulty functioning because the darkness is so intense. Their only motivation for continuing to be faithful is that their efforts may somehow help others. During her darkest moments, Mother Teresa wrote that her only relief came when she was with the poor. Only there did she find Jesus. And yet, one gets the impression from her writings that this awareness was not experienced as consolation, but as a temporary reprieve from her suffering.

Some lay ministers may seek relief from the midnight darkness in the active apostolate, similar to the way Mother Teresa experienced relief in being with the poor. Others may long to relinquish their responsibilities as conflicts within the sphere of ministry intensify their doubts. Surrounded by darkness, they hold onto prayer the way a drowning person would cling to a raft, despite the fact that prayer is void of consolation. Not unlike the child who is exhausted and overcome by the horrors of a nightmare, those in the night of spirit surrender in faith to God as their only refuge, despite the feeling that even God has rejected them.

Using the imagery of the prophet Ezekiel, John of the Cross used the analogy of fire: "For the prophet asserts that in order to burn away the rust of the affections, the soul must, as it were, be annihilated and undone in the measure that these passions and imperfections are connatural to it."[3]

The longing of these souls for God becomes more intense. Despite the lack of consolation, they remain faithful to prayer and good works, regardless of the outcome. Their individual needs become insignificant compared to the needs of others. The suffering of others now becomes an extension of their interior pain. Watching the news can evoke tears as their hearts are united with the pain of the suffering Body of Christ. The more their will is united to the will of God, the more their love and concern embrace all of humanity.

Again John of the Cross helps us to understand how this can be so. "And my will departed from itself and became divine. United with the divine love, it no longer loves in a lowly manner, with its natural strength, but with the strength and purity of the Holy Spirit; and thus the will does not operate humanly in relation to God."[4]

When souls are released from this type of darkness (and it may be only temporarily) the initial relief experienced is sometimes likened to an exorcism, for it seems that the soul has escaped the powers of hell.

The more persons are united to the will of God, the more they are willing to relinquish their own will. As they are stripped of self-serving inclinations, perseverance is no longer dependent on specific outcomes. Although they work tirelessly, the focus becomes the sacredness of each moment. Consecration of the process allows them to view their efforts with a holy indifference about the perceived success of a project.

When it looked as if a house that St. Teresa was working to establish would not come to fruition, the saint neither fretted nor attacked those who stood in her way. While she left no stone unturned in regard to the effort, her attitude remained one of surrender. She understood that in the end God would prevail and she accepted whatever happened with perfect resignation. As the level of surrender to God increases, so does the understanding of lay ministers who realize that they are but a small part of Jesus' mission to build the Kingdom of God. Teresa's example invites all who journey in faith to embrace every person in a spirit of charity, even those with whom they may disagree. Lay ecclesial ministers can learn from the high priority that Teresa placed on obedience. She remained obedient to her superiors and to the institutional Church even though she did not always agree with those in authority. Teresa saw God's will for her on earth in the voice of her superiors. And at the end of her life, she found great joy in dying as a daughter of the Church.

Saints who in their lifetime brought about reform rarely started out with reform as their goal. They were led to such paths in the course of a more humble effort, while never losing sight of the need to deepen their relationship with God. These saints grew into their roles as reformers, trusting that it was God who was leading them. Their lives validate the Parable of the Talents. Those who remained faithful during the master's absence were rewarded. Recall that upon the master's return he said, "...you were faithful in small matters, I will give you great responsibilities. Come, share your master's joy" (Mt 25:23). Spiritual growth is accompanied by a willingness to serve God, even at great personal cost. Those who follow this path trust that God's hidden grace is leading and guiding them to further His kingdom. As ministers journey in faith, God leads them along a path that is replete with both the joys and sorrows.

Mary's fiat offers a perfect example of faith in the presence of tremendous obstacles. The union of Mary's will with the will of God was the cause of great joy but it also brought sorrow, causing her heart to feel as if it were pierced by a sword. Through it all, Mary remained faithful. She opened her heart and surrendered her life to God. Her journey took her from the security of her home in Nazareth to a stable in Bethlehem. It meant fleeing to Egypt, seeking Jesus when He was lost and eventually climbing the hill to Calvary. In the presence of uncertainty, she did what every contemplative does: She pondered in her heart that which she did not understand. Mary remained open to the wisdom of God in the face of chaos and horrendous sorrow. Every action was inspired by God. Through the perfect surrender of her will to the will of God, Mary remains the perfect model for all who seek to do the will of God in the midst of the unknown.

JOURNALING QUESTIONS

1. How has my faith been tested in my prayer life?
2. In what ways has my faith been tested in external trials of life?
3. Have I ever felt abandoned by God?
4. Do I pray more or less when I experience turmoil and heartache?
5. What kinds of situations have humbled me?
6. How do I typically respond to such humbling circumstances?
7. How do I respond when assailed by doubts?
8. How has grace brought me through experiences of darkness?

CHAPTER XI

GOD'S HIDDEN COMMUNICATION

IN SECRET AND IN DARKNESS

To help understand God's hidden communication during the night of the spirit, Zechariah's experience in the temple once again offers a way to illustrate what is taking place in the soul of those who are brought to this level of darkness. When Zechariah entered the sanctuary, he was no longer visible to the people who waited for him in the assembly. According to the Gospel account, Zechariah's prolonged absence led the people to wonder why he was taking so long. At the time, they had no idea that an angel of the Lord was conversing with him since those who waited outside were not privy to the communication that was taking place inside.

Not unlike the people who waited outside the sanctuary unaware of what was happening, the senses are not privy to supernatural communications from God. While the senses act as a gateway to the soul, they are not able to enter the inner sanctum of the soul. Just as the people remained in darkness during Zechariah's encounter with the angel, so the senses are kept in the dark when God communes with the soul on a supernatural level. We know from Scripture that when Zechariah emerged, he was unable to speak. Only then did the people realize that something extraordinary had taken place. Still, they knew nothing about the specifics of Zechariah's encounter with God.

John of the Cross tells us that the more interior and spiritual the divine communication, the darker and more obscure the encounter appears to sensory perception. Just as those who try to gaze into the sun are blinded by the brilliance of its light, so the memory and the intellect are blinded by the brilliance of God's love when God communes with the soul in this manner.

During the illuminative stage and early, transient experiences of union, God may communicate his presence through the senses in the form of visions, locutions or other sensory phenomena. However, not all who journey toward union experience such phenomena. God draws each person according to His will, and the presence of somatic or sensory phenomena is not a guarantee that the soul is experiencing the prayer of union.

Both John and Teresa maintain that the mind, emotions and the devil can cause such phenomena, deluding persons into believing they are receiving divine communications when in reality human frailty or the devil may actually be the cause of their experience. The adage, "by their fruits you will know them" is a more reliable indicator by which to validate the gift of union. When God is truly at work in the heart and life of persons who open themselves to His grace, virtue and goodness are the result.

St. Teresa talks about the faculties being put to sleep during prayer and, indeed, it seems as if the intellect is anesthetized. In discussing God's hidden communication during the night of the senses, I used the analogy of restorative sleep. During the night of the spirit, sleep induced by anesthesia seems more descriptive of the soul's experience. The senses are seized with such force that resistance is impossible. The intellect is rendered helpless and is placed in a passive and totally receptive mode. Just as a person is unable to resist the effects of an anesthetizing drug by willing it, so a person is helpless to resist the power of God that invades the soul during the night of the spirit. When the intellect is put to sleep, the will is captivated. To understand what is transpiring in the spiritual life during this stage, we once again turn to John of the Cross.

> That the soul with its faculties be divinely tempered and prepared for the divine union of love, it must first be engulfed in this divine and dark spiritual light of contemplation, and thereby be withdrawn from all creature affections and apprehensions. The duration of this absorption is proportionate to the intensity of the contemplation. The more simply and purely the divine light strikes the soul, the more it darkens and empties and annihilates it in its particular apprehensions and affections concerning both earthly and heavenly things; and, also, the less simply and purely it shines, the less it deprives and darkens the soul.[1]

All that remains is the quiet of "unknowing," which persons experiencing the phenomenon are at a loss to explain except that its origin is divine. Understandably, these divine encounters are met with fear and trepidation. Initially, the mind may try to resist. But the force of the spirit is such that the memory and intellect of those who experience God's self-communication in this manner are rendered helpless.

Turning once again to Zechariah to provide an analogy, we know that when he emerged from the sanctuary unable to speak, the people outside were at a loss to explain what was beyond their natural ability to comprehend. Nevertheless, neither he nor those who were in the assembly could dismiss what had taken place as the product of an overactive imagination. Although they were left wondering about the specifics of this wondrous encounter, Zechariah had been left mute and that provided tangible evidence that something extraordinary had happened. Then, as the events surrounding Elizabeth's pregnancy played out in the months that followed, all marveled at what had taken place.

In drawing a comparison with God's hidden communication during the night of the spirit, an increase of virtue and a tireless dedication to the will of God serve as indicators that something has taken place in the depths of the soul, despite the lack of awareness on a sensory or intellectual level.

A BLINDING LIGHT

Persons experiencing God's touch on a deeply spiritual level are unable to understand what has transpired. In the absence of sensory involvement, only darkness prevails, accompanied by a sense of unknowing regarding what has occurred. "I do not know" or "I cannot explain it" seem to be common responses by those who find there are neither words nor mental constructs that can aptly describe their experience. There may also be a sense of timelessness. What seems like seconds may actually take place over a period of thirty minutes or an hour.

The experience of a person waking up from anesthesia is an apt comparison. The sleep that is induced is not the result of natural fatigue. Likewise, contemplation or the infused presence of God cannot be brought about by one's own effort. We can dispose ourselves to God's action deep within our soul, but we cannot cause it. Prior to surgery, the last memory of those being put to sleep is that of the drug being administered in the operating room. Then, in what seems like seconds later, they awaken only to discover that a much longer period of time has elapsed and that the surgery is over. Just as the memory has no recollection of what transpired when the person undergoing surgery was asleep, so during a deeply spiritual communication the memory has no intellectual knowledge of the soul's experience.

John explains how the intellect and memory are kept in darkness by drawing a comparison about natural light and dust particles that are observed when light passes through a window. "The reason is that light in itself is invisible and is rather the means by which the object it strikes is seen; but it is also seen when it reflects on them."[2] Since light is invisible, it is only seen as it reflects on that which stands in its path. In the absence of such obstructions vis-à-vis imperfections, light is experienced by the intellect as darkness. And since that which separates the person from the will of God has been removed, the experience of God, who is absolute Light, is experienced as darkness. As John points out:

> The cause for not experiencing these agreeable effects is the soul's weakness and the imperfection at the time, its inadequate preparation, and the qualities it possesses which are contrary to this light. Because of these, the soul has to suffer when the divine light shines upon it."[3]

God's hidden communication by-passes the senses and as a result, those who experience the dark night of spirit experience only the seeming absence of God. Recipients of such infused touches of grace are reduced to a sense of their own sinfulness. Consequently, suffering is embraced without question or hesitation as it seems that punishment is all they deserve. Feelings of consolation can actually contribute to the suffering experienced by those at this stage of union with God. A heightened awareness of the deep chasm between humanity and divinity contributes to a sense of unworthiness, which instills a preference for anonymity. Praise and adulation intensify the suffering as these persons see only their own nothingness in relation to the magnitude and holiness of God. Divine favors, when experienced, become a source of deep shame and caused some saints to ask they not receive them.

At times those in the dark night feel as though they are on the brink of despair, as all seems lost. And yet they persevere, led by the Spirit that continues to hide its presence even as God guides these persons through the sea of darkness. This process has been described by Abbott Thomas Keating as "divine therapy." He explains that the psyche is healed on a deeper level where human access is impossible and has as its goal transformation of the intellect and will through grace.[4] This healing process can be likened to a person who undergoes a surgical procedure. While in this state, God removes remaining attachments to sin that are so deeply embedded in the person's being that only God can reach.

The path to permanent union or the spiritual marriage is a process that requires healing from the inside out. In order for deep cleansing and healing to take place, all remnants of the false self must be stripped away. Just as a person awakens from surgery and experiences pain, so the wound of love that God inflicts on the soul leaves it longing ever more intensely for God. And yet, so mindful is this person of their sinfulness that they feel God has truly abandoned them and is justified in doing so. It is purgatory on earth for those so afflicted, but in the process persons who are united to God in the night of the spirit are being transformed into His image without conscious awareness of themselves. This darkness of unknowing only amplifies the torment. The writings of Mother Teresa provide insight into this seeming paradox.

> Lord, my God, who am I that you should forsake me? The child of your love – and now becomes as the most hated one – the one You have thrown away as unwanted – unloved. I call, I cling, I want – and there is no One to answer – no One on Whom I can cling – no, No One, - Alone. The darkness is so dark – and I am alone. – Unwanted, forsaken.[5]

John's analogy of a log that is consumed by the fire illustrates the oneness of the union through which these souls journey. "Fire when first applied to wood, first dehumidifies it, dispelling all moisture and making it give off all water it contains. Then it gradually turns the wood dark and ugly, and even causes it to emit a bad odor."[6] As attachment to other affections is burned away, union with God becomes the heart's sole desire. Ignited by the fire of God's love, the soul witnesses the vileness of sin as these bad humors escape when touched by God. This explains why so many saints considered themselves terrible sinners even though they were living what most would consider very virtuous lives.

Blinded by the presence of God's love, those at this stage of the journey are deprived of any satisfaction that could console them. Since they experience only the absence of God, they believe that God has abandoned them. Yet, love cannot be contained. Consequently, the thirst of persons so consumed by God's burning love seeks an outlet. It is not surprising that they are tireless in their effort to share what they have come to know as the goodness of God. Enkindled by the love that now consumes them, they become single-minded in their desire to love and serve God. Regardless of the consequences, their lives echo the words of Jesus during His agony in the Garden of Olives, "Abba, Father, all things are possible to you. Take this cup away from me, but not what I will but what you will." (Mk 14:36).

The real proof of union lies in the effects that are produced by the night of the spirit. Deeper levels of love, compassion and humility prevail beyond the prayer experience. With their focus blinded by the light of God's love, those in this night do not perceive their own goodness. Rather than being deceived by false humility, they have such an abhorrence of sin that it may sound like self-deprecation to others. Many saints had become so sensitive to the vileness of sin that any remaining impurities they beheld in themselves caused a deep sorrow because of the great chasm that sin created between God and the human person.

The great paradox of the night of the spirit is that all the while these souls are being sorely tried God is flooding their soul with His divine light and love.

MINISTRY AT ITS FINEST

When ministers in the active apostolate look for a model, St. Therese of Lisieux provides a good example. Her "little way of love," which is sometimes dismissed because of its simplicity, is a culmination of all that St. John of the Cross and St. Teresa of Avila hoped to provide for those who seek a deep and loving relationship with God. This should come as no surprise. As a Carmelite, St. Therese was familiar with the teachings of these two great saints and was particularly attracted to the writings of John of the Cross.

Rather than being sanguine or childish as some wrongly conclude, the writings of St. Therese offer an insight into the dark night which was very much a part of her faith journey. In the absence of consolation, her decision to smile and accept all as gift is sometimes mistaken as naiveté. But only the spiritually mature are able to take up their cross without complaining. The image she used of her being a rubber ball that the child Jesus could play with or cast aside as He willed provides a window into the abandonment to the will of God that directed Therese's life. It is an example of the holy indifference to feelings of consolation that typify the resolve of those who embrace the dark night of spirit. To the outsider, who is not privy to the interior torment of these souls, difficult situations appear to be less of a burden than they actually are. But it is the decision to love God and others in the presence of what feels like purgatory that makes seemingly ordinary individuals reach the heights of sanctity.

As the darkness continues, it is not surprising that the interior life becomes more real than external matters. Those who are drawn into the night of spirit appreciate more than ever the passing nature of sensory and spiritual attachments. As their longing for God increases, so does their longing for others to know God. Truly, this is ministry at its finest.

The more souls are united with God, the more they are transformed. On a very intrinsic level, they long for others to experience what they have come to know. With hearts focused on God, they pay little attention to the sorrow that is embedded in their experience of abandonment. And so they live the Gospel mandate, "…whoever wishes to come after me must deny himself, take up his cross, and follow me" (Mt 17:24). All is for the sake of the Kingdom. They are willing to drink from the chalice of love for the sake of others, bitter though it may be. Clearly, it could be no other way, for the path to union is not an exclusive journey. Contemplative prayer and the active apostolate share two things in common: neither are a "God and I" journey, nor are they mutually exclusive.

While the journey to God may begin with self-love, it cannot remain there when hearts are open to God's grace. Those who continue the journey are transformed from a "me-centered" mentality to a "God-centered" offering of their life. Every effort is put forth in the name of God, out of love for God and for the sanctity of the human family.

Teresa of Avila explains, "The Lord asks of us only two things: love of His Majesty and love of our neighbor. These are what we must work for."[7] She goes on to counsel that since we cannot know whether or not we love God, we can only judge our love for God by the manner with which we love our neighbor.

Just as John of the Cross is known for his analogy of the log that is consumed and becomes one with the fire during the prayer of union, so Teresa uses the analogy of the butterfly to describe the interior and exterior disposition during these later stages of the spiritual journey. She uses the image of the silk worm that dies in the cocoon and emerges like a butterfly that flits about and is always bearing fruit. In her description of a person at this stage, Teresa wrote, "Although it is always bearing fruit by doing good for itself and for other souls, it never stops to rest, because it fails to find its true repose."[8]

As persons draw closer to God, they work tirelessly for the salvation of souls. Here active ministry and the contemplative life become fused as both the minister and the contemplative die to self. Again we turn to Teresa for an explanation. The saint counseled her sisters, "…let us desire and be occupied in prayer not for the sake of our enjoyment but so as to have the strength to serve."[9] The saint further instructs her sisters:

> Believe me, Martha and Mary must join together to show hospitality to the Lord and have Him always present and not host Him badly by failing to give Him something to eat. How would Mary, always seated at His feet, provide Him with food if her sister did not help her? His food is that in every way we draw souls that they may be saved and praise Him always.[10]

Teresa refuted the objection that Mary had chosen the better part by saying that Mary had already performed the task of Martha by washing the feet of Jesus and enduring the humiliation by the Pharisees. Although recent scholarship disclaims the notion that Mary and the woman who washed the feet of Jesus are the same person, the message Teresa conveys is that the real work of the spiritual life is purification. And the spiritual marriage cannot take place until this work is accomplished.

The degree of union that a soul experiences is directly related to the level of purification that takes place, and purification is the work of the interior life. It prepares the soul for the various stages of union with God and, if God wills, brings the person into the spiritual marriage. So it is that Martha and Mary depend on one another. Rather than one being opposed to the other, they work together so that persons may be transformed into the image of God who created the world and rested on the seventh day.

Always the practical spiritual guide, Teresa understood the value of work and cautioned her sisters about the dangers of confusing prayer with idleness. She viewed work as a means to grow closer to God, not as an end in itself. The saint admonished her sisters not to build castles in the air, dreaming of grandiose ways to serve the Lord. Lest they confuse work with great accomplishments she wrote, "The Lord doesn't look so much at the greatness of our works as at the love with which they are done."[11]

These are words that every minister can take to heart. When plans go awry; when the turnout for adult education sessions is far less than expected; when good intentions are misinterpreted, and when obstacles seem endless, it is easy to question the worth and even the wisdom behind the effort. But as long as ministers treat each person with kindness and respect and put forth an honest effort to further the Kingdom of God by offering all to Him, then nothing is lost.

When, despite their best effort, those who labor in the vineyard receive nothing tangible in return for their effort yet continue to serve their brothers and sisters in Christ, they are experiencing the night of the spirit and the benefits are unlimited. When the yearning to be one in Christ culminates in a willingness to be blessed and broken, lay ministers reflect the love of Jesus who on the night before He died prayed that all might be one in Him as He and the Father are one.

The closer one grows to God, the more a person seeks God in a selfless manner. Although the personal cost is high and God's loving self-communication remains obscure, hearts are consumed by the desire to seek him out, not for their own satisfaction, but to please God. John describes this posture as habitual and wearisome suffering when it sees not all are consumed with the same desire. This sorrow deep within causes the heart to cry out:

> Ah, my Lord and my God! How many go to you looking for their own consolation and gratification and desiring that You grant them favors and gifts, but those wanting to give You pleasure and something at cost to themselves, setting aside their own interests, are few. What is lacking is not that You, O my God, desire to grant us favors again, but that we make use of them for Your service alone and thus oblige You to grant them to us continually.[12]

This purified love causes persons to be imbued with the virtues of faith, hope and charity. With the spiritual appetites stilled, a habitual state of quietude allows souls who have reached this remarkable state of purity to rest even in their sorrow. It is the disposition of those graced souls who have made their home in the heart of God. John of the Cross explains, "…love alone, which at this period burns by soliciting the heart for the Beloved, is what guides and moves it and makes it soar to God in an unknown way along the road of solitude."[13] At this stage, hearts will echo the words of John of the Cross whose own heart rejoiced.

> On that glad night,
> In secret, for no one saw me,
> Nor did I look at anything,
> With no other light or guide
> Than the one that burned in my heart.[14]

JOURNALING QUESTIONS

1. Have I felt abandoned by God?
2. If yes, what precipitated it and how did I respond?
3. Did the experience weaken or strengthen my resolve?
4. What did I learn from it?
5. What does this tell me about God's hidden communication during the night of the spirit?
6. If I have not experienced the dark night, what feelings does reading this chapter evoke?
7. What are the obstacles that deter me from making progress in the spiritual life?
8. What steps can I take to prepare myself to surrender my will to the will of God?

CONCLUSION

Both Sts. Teresa and John of the Cross maintain that although many begin the journey to union, few reach it in their lifetime. After reading the previous chapters, you can well appreciate why this is so. The path to union is not a path that is embarked upon by the faint of heart. Some might wonder why anyone would embrace a path where suffering and unknowing seem to be present at almost every turn. The answer may lie, in part, in the words of the psalmist who wrote, "[b]etter one day in your courts than a thousand elsewhere" (Ps 84:11). They are words that could only have been prompted by a personal experience of union with God. In looking back, the psalmist decided that the ecstasy was well worth the agony. Similarly, Paul's reassurance "[w]hat eye has not seen, and ear has not heard, and what has not entered the human heart, what God has prepared for those who love him" (1 Cor 2:9) could only have been spoken because he experienced union with God on a deep and profound level.

St. Augustine echoed similar sentiments when he wrote, "You have made us for yourself, and our heart is restless until it rests in you."[1] We are created to find union with God. The journey is fraught with obstacles that each person has been given a lifetime to overcome and every person does so with a greater or lesser degree of success.

The Catholic Church teaches that by virtue of our Baptism, we are all called to be saints. As the late Archbishop Dom Helder Camara, whose uncompromising commitment to the poor won him the admiration of many, wrote:

> In the last analysis, sanctity is nothing but the Lord. He invites us to share in his holiness. But this shared holiness is neither an entitlement to glory nor a privilege reserved for exceptional souls, and much less a favor that we want to offer God. It is an obligation for all of us from the moment, through Baptism, we receive the sanctifying grace that makes us holy.[2]

Who should understand our Baptismal calling better than those who labor in the vineyard of the Lord? It could be said that lay ministers have been doubly called. They have been chosen in a unique way as disciples and apostles, but unless lay ministry is built on the call to an ever deepening relationship with God, both ministers and their apostolate are at risk.

Some church leaders recognize that intentional spiritual formation of lay ministers has been sorely neglected. Too often, spiritual formation has been sacrificed for the sake of continuing education. Attending conferences may take precedence over making a retreat or attending to matters of spiritual development, but it should not be a choice that requires selecting one over the other. Both are essential. With an ever increasing number of lay ministers filling staff positions in parishes and dioceses, more time, attention and resources are needed for the ongoing spiritual formation of the laity. In order for ministers to evangelize effectively, they must also be evangelized. And evangelization involves ongoing conversion through a commitment to a disciplined prayer life.

Recall the question, "so how is your prayer life?" posed in chapter one. It remains a valid question. Hopefully, reflecting on the writings of John and Teresa has given you a deeper appreciation for the role of prayer in your life and in ministry. The importance of prayer cannot be overstated, for when ministers lose sight of prayer as a way to deepen their relationship with God, everyone suffers. Simply stated, the gaze of lay ministers must be directed both inward and outward, integrating the heart with the head and the hands.

Burnout continues to be a common phenomenon among ministers and for many who work in the people-serving professions. This need not be the case if we take advantage of the experience and guidance of those who have traveled the road before us. Ministers today face the same challenges that the saints overcame. Their wisdom has withstood the test of time and provides insight that still applies today. While the thought of turning back is always an option, it holds little attraction for those who have fallen in love with God. Even when persons feel called in another direction or retire from active ministry, the journey to union with God continues, for the call to holiness outlives every other role and responsibility. It is the end for which we are all created.

When the apostles dropped everything to follow Jesus, they could not have known that all but one would die a martyr's death. Each one grew into the role of apostle, martyr and saint. The same holds true for us. Times and circumstances are different, but the journey to divine union demands the same type of radical love.

In the *Living Flame of Love,* John of the Cross warned his readers that God cannot fill an occupied heart. From the very beginning, the Christian journey has been about the union of wills. From the cave in Bethlehem to the cross on Calvary, we know that union with God does not come without a cost. Yet, all too often, we, like Adam, believe the great lie that tells us that we can have God on our own terms. With eyes too blind to see, we try to use God to fulfill our dream. And, in the process, we create a god that resembles our image and likeness. This will never do. In the "*Spiritual Canticle*," John lamented:

> Many desire that God cost them no more than words, and even these they say badly. They scarcely desire to do anything for Him that might cost them some-

> thing. Some would not even rise from a place of their liking, if they were not able to receive some delight from God in their mouth and heart. They will not even take one step to mortify themselves and loose some of their satisfactions and comforts. Unless they go in search of God they will not find Him, no matter how much they cry for Him.[3]

The journey to union demands that all false idols be destroyed and addictions overcome. The darkness serves as a reminder that the Kingdom of God will come only when hearts that have erected temples to the false gods are destroyed. For ministers, that means seeking God before we attend to plans, programs and projects. It means directing a kind word to the person who challenges us every step of the way, and it means letting go of expectations. But, most of all, it means setting aside time to be still and allow God to direct our life.

The active apostolate cannot thrive unless it is rooted in a contemplative heart. It is the irony that led St. Therese, the Little Flower of Carmel, to be designated Patroness of the Foreign Missions. Although she never left the cloister and died at the age of twenty-four, she has been named a Doctor of the Church. In her autobiography she related how she lamented the fact that she could not be an apostle or prophet or teacher - that is - until she realized she could be all of them. Upon reading St. Paul's discourse on love in chapter thirteen of Corinthians, chapter thirteen she wrote:

> I understood that the Church had a heart and that this heart was burning with Love. I understood that it was Love alone that made the Church's members act, that if Love ever became extinct, apostles would not preach the Gospel and martyrs would not shed their blood. I understood that Love comprised all vocations, that love was everything, and that it embraced all times and places…in a word it was eternal.[4]

St. Therese understood that the hands of the Church cannot function apart from its heart. It is the heart that transforms ministers into contemplatives and contemplatives into ministers. As each ascends the mountain of the Lord, they will discover that the path to union involves the marriage of the active and contemplative life. Consummate union holds nothing back. Every thought, word and action is directed to the One whose love knows no bounds. And therein lies the secret. The spiritual marriage is nothing more than the total surrender of a person's will to the object of their heart's desire. And while such heroic generosity is impossible to achieve by human effort alone, with God all things are possible.

ENDNOTES

In referring works by St. John of the Cross, the citation contains three numbers. The first number indicates the book, the second number the chapter and the third number the section. For example, *AMC*, 2.5.3 refers to *The Ascent of Mount Carmel*, second book, chapter five, section three.

In referring to *The Interior Castle*, the first number indicates the number of the Dwelling Place, the second number the chapter and the third number the section (*IC*, 7.4.6). In *The Way of Perfection*, the work has only two numbers indicating chapter and section.

FOREWORD

1. John of the Cross, *The Ascent of Mount of Carmel*, in *The Collected Works of St. John of the Cross* , trans. Kieran Kavanaugh, OCD and Otilio Rodriguez, OCD (Washington DC: ISC Publications, 1991), 2.7.11.
2. Ibid.
3. John of the Cross, letter no. 5 to Madre Ana de San Alberto in Caravaca, from Sevilla, June 1586, in *The Collected Works of St. Teresa of Avila,* vol.2, trans. Kieran Kavanaugh, OCD and Otilio Rodriguez, OCD (Washington DC: ISC Publications, 1979), 738.
4. John of the Cross, *The Dark Night*, in *The Collected Works of St. John of the Cross,* bk. 2, trans. Kieran Kavanaugh, OCD and Otilio Rodriguez, OCD (Washington DC: ISC Publications, 1979), 2.4.1-2.

CHAPTER I - CALLED TO RELATIONSHIP

1. Bernard of Clairvaux, *Bernard of Clairvaux: A Lover Teaching the Way of Love*, ed. M. Basil Pennington (New York: New City Press, 1997), 103.
2. Augustine, *The Confessions,* trans. John K. Ryan (Garden City, New York: Image Books, 1960), 43.
3. John of the Cross, *The Spiritual Canticle,* in *The Collected Works of St. John of the Cross,* trans. Kieran Kavanaugh, OCD and Otilio Rodriguez, OCD (Washington DC: ISC Publications, 1979), 12.7.
4. Ibid., 2.5.3.
5. Leonard Doohan, *The Contemporary Challenge of John of the Cross* (Washington, D.C.: ISC Publications, 1995), 78.
6. John of the Cross, *Spiritual Canticle*, 29.3.
7. Committee on the Laity of the USCCB, *Co-Workers in the Vineyard of the Lord,* (Washington DC: USCCB, 2005), 39.
8. John of the Cross, *Dark Night*, 7.4.6.

9. Brother Lawrence of the Resurrection, *The Practice of the Presence of God,* trans. John J. Delaney (New York: Image Book, Doubleday,1977), 11.
10. Thomas Merton, *Thomas Merton: Disputed Questions* (New York: Harcourt, 1985), 178.
11. Ibid., 178.
12. John of the Cross, *Dark Night*, 2.13.7.
13. John of the Cross, 31.1.

CHAPTER II – ROMANCE

1. Merton, *Disputed Questions*, 105.
2. Ibid., 106.
3. John of the Cross, *Dark Night*, 1. 2.2.
4. Doohan, *Contemporary Challenge*, 21.
5. Ibid., 21.
6. John of the Cross, *Dark Night*, 1.2.8.
7. Thomas Merton, *Thoughts in Solitude,* rev. ed. (New York: Farrar, Straus and Giroux, 1984), 43.

CHAPTER III – DISILLUSIONMENT

1. Bernard of Clairvaux, *Teaching the Way*, 107.
2. John of the Cross, *Dark Night*, 1.1.3.
3. John of the Cross, *Ascent of Mount of Carmel*, 1.12.3.
4. Ibid. 1.4.5.
5. Teresa of Avila, *The Interior Castle* in *The Collected Works of St. Teresa of Avila,* vol.2, trans. Kieran Kavanaugh, OCD and Otilio Rodriguez, OCD (Washington DC: ISC Publications, 1980), Epilogue, 2.
6. John of the Cross, *Dark Night*, 1.2.1.
7. Mother Teresa of Calcutta, *Thirsting for God: Mother Teresa's Yearbook of Prayers, Meditations and Anecdotes for the Third Millennium* (Cincinnati: Servant Publications, 2000), 88.
8. Teresa of Avila, *The Way of Perfection,* in *The Collected Works of St. Teresa of Avila,* vol.2, trans. Kieran Kavanaugh, OCD and Otilio Rodriguez, OCD (Washington DC: ISC Publications, 1979), Introduction, 31.
9. John of the Cross, *Ascent of Mount Carmel,* 2.18.2.
10. Ibid 1.13.5.
11. Edith Stein, *The Science of the Cross* (Washington DC: ICS Publications, 2003), 37.

CHAPTER IV – THE FOOT OF THE MOUNTAIN

1. Teresa of Avila, *Interior Castle,* 1.2.7.
2. John of the Cross, "The Poetry," in *The Collected Works of St. John of the Cross,* rev. ed., trans. Kieran Kavanaugh, OCD and Otilio Rodriguez, OCD (Washington DC: ISC Publications, 1991), 113-14.
3. Ibid., 113-14.

CHAPTER V – MORTIFICATION OF THE SENSES

1. John of the Cross, *Ascent of Mount of Carmel*, 1.8.4.
2. Ibid., 1.4.4.
3. Ibid., 1.6.1.
4. Ibid., 1.8.4.65.
5. Bernard of Clairvaux, *Selected Works of Bernard of Clairvaux* (Harper Collins: San Francisco. 2005), 8.
6. Henri J.M. Nouwen, *The Return of the Prodigal Son* (New York: Image Books Doubleday, 1992), Prologue.
7. John of the Cross, *Dark Night*, 1.2.1.
8. Ibid., 1.2.4.
9. Francis of Assisi, *Prayer for Peace.*
10. John of the Cross, *Ascent of Mount Carmel,* 1.13.11.

CHAPTER VI – JOURNEYING IN FAITH

1. John of the Cross, *Dark Night*, 1.8.3.
2. Teresa of Avila, *Interior Castle*, 3.2.2.
3. Stein, *Science of the Cross,* 52.
4. Merton, *Thoughts in Solitude*, 83.

CHAPTER VII – GOD'S HIDDEN COMMUNICATION

1. John of the Cross, *Dark Night*, 1.13.1.
2. Ibid., 1.12.4.
3. Ibid., 1.13.3.
4. Ibid., 1.12. 4.
5. Teresa of Avila, *Interior Castle*, 3.1.9.
6. John of the Cross, *Dark Night*, 1.12.4.
7. Ibid., 1.13.12-13.
8. Ibid., 1.14.3.

CHAPTER VIII – THE ILLUMINATIVE STAGE

1. John of the Cross, *Ascent of Mount of Carmel*, 2.14.2.
2. John of the Cross, *Dark Night*, 2.1.1.
3. Ibid., 2.2.3.
4. Teresa of Avila, *Interior Castle,* 4.2.9.
5. James B. Dunning, *Ministries: Sharing God's Gifts* (Terrace Heights, MN: St. Mary's Press, 1980), 89.
6. Johannes Baptist Metz, *Poverty of Spirit*, trans. John Drury (New York, NY: Paulist Press, 1968), 14.
7. Ibid., 16-17.
8. Ibid., 19.
9. John of the Cross, *Dark Night*, 2.3.1.

CHAPTER IX – DYING TO THE SENSES

1. John of the Cross, *Dark Night*, 2.2.1.
2. Ibid., 2.2.2.
3. Ibid., 2.4.2.
4. Ibid., 2.6.2-3.
5. Ibid., 2.6.5.

CHAPTER X - JOURNEYING IN FAITH

1. John of the Cross, *Ascent of Mount of Carmel*, 2.1.1.
2. Ibid., 2.7.3.
3. Ibid., 2.6.5.
4. Ibid., 2.4.2.

CHAPTER XI – GOD'S HIDDEN COMMUNICATION

1. John of the Cross, *Ascent of Mount of Carmel*, 2.8.2.
2. Ibid., 2.8.3.
3. Ibid., 2.9.11.
4. Thomas Keating, "Psychology and the Spiritual Journey," *Contemplative Outreach News* 22:1 (December 2006), 16.
5. Mother Teresa of Calcutta, *Mother Teresa: Come Be My Light: The Private Writings of the Saint of Calcutta* (New York: Doubleday, 2007), 186-87.
6. John of the Cross, *Dark Night,* 2.10.1.
7. Teresa of Avila, *Interior Castle*, 5.3.7.
8. Ibid., 5.4.2.
9. Ibid., 7.4.12.
10. Ibid., 7.4.12
11. Ibid., 7.4.15.
12. John of the Cross, *Dark Night,* 2.19.4.
13. Ibid., 2.25.4.
14. John of the Cross, *Ascent of Mount of Carmel*, 2.25, stanza 3.

CONCLUSION

1. Augustine, *The Confessions,* trans. John K. Ryan (Garden City, New York: Image Books, 1960), 1.1.43.
2. Conrad De Meester, *With Empty Hands* (Washington, DC: ICS Publications, 2002), Introduction, x.
3. John of the Cross, *Spiritual Canticle,* commentary on stanza 3.2.
4. Therese of Lisieux, *Story of a Soul*, 3d ed. trans. John Clarke (Washington, DC: ICS Publications, 1996), 194.

GLOSSARY

Contemplation – according to the Carmelite tradition, the application of the term is reserved for the description of infused prayer, which is regarded as a supernatural favor granted to persons who seek union with God through interior prayer. The broader, and perhaps more common usage of the term, refers to a method of prayer that has become synonymous with meditation or quiet reflection. The narrow application refers to God's action in the depth of the human heart; the broader meaning includes human effort involved in the practice of interior prayer.

Discursive meditation – the practice of reflecting on Scripture or a religious theme or person which actively engages the imaginations and intellect.

Illuminative way – the second stage of the threefold path. It serves as a transitional stage between the night of sense and the night of spirit. This stage provides encouragement and somewhat of a reprieve before encountering a deeper level of purification. This marks the beginning of infused prayer, which is a supernatural favor from God.

Mental prayer – the practice of quiet listening with loving attentiveness to the indwelling presence of God.

Mystical – used to describe a transformative experience that results in a conscious awareness of the presence of God's love and is associated with deepening levels of infused prayer. The experience is a gift from God and cannot be acquired by human effort.

Mystical Marriage – a metaphor used to describe the highest level of union between God and a person. It is the highest level of interior transformation and reflects perfect alignment of the human will with God's will. All the mystics agree that few are brought to this permanent state of union in this life.

Purgative way – the beginning of the threefold path of the spiritual journey that invites persons to faithful living and to overcome disordered attachments as a way to cleanse their hearts in preparation for a deeper experience of God's love.

Soul – the interior part of the human person that is other than body and which animates the entire being. Soul is always God's creation, but it is within the realm of each person to awaken it by seeing all things and every event in God. John of the Cross uses the word soul in reference to a person who is engaged in doing the work required to awaken the soul to the presence of God.

Threefold path – a term used to describe the three stages of the interior life that dates back to the third century. The purgative, illuminative and unitive stages are usually developmental, but they are also fluid. Therefore spiritual travelers continue to experience deepening levels of purgation even during the unitive stages of the spiritual journey.

Unitive way – the third stage, which is considered the way of the perfect, is dominated by the love of God. Having reached a higher level of transformation, those in the unitive stage see God in all things. Key to the unitive stage is a transformation of the will as it becomes more deeply aligned with the will of God.

BIBLIOGRAPHY

Augustine. *The Confessions of St. Augustine*. Translated by John K. Ryan. Garden City, New York: Image Books, 1960.

Bernard of Clairvaux. *Bernard of Clairvaux: A Lover Teaching the Way of Love*. Edited by M. Basil Pennington. New York: New City Press, 1997.

Bernard of Clairvaux: Selected Works. Edited by Emilie Griffin. San Francisco: Harper Collins, 2005.

Co-Workers in the Vineyard of the Lord. Washington DC: United States Conference of Catholic Bishops, 2005.

De Meester, Conrad. *With Empty Hands*. Washington, DC: ICS Publications, 2002.

Doohan, Leonard. *The Contemporary Challenge of John of the Cross*. Washington, DC: ISC Publications, 1995.

Dunning, James B. *Ministries: Sharing God's Gifts*. Terrace Heights, Minnesota: St. Mary's Press, 1980.

John of the Cross. *The Ascent of Mount Carmel*. In *The Collected Works of St. John of the Cross*. Translated by Kieran Kavanaugh, OCD and Otilio Rodriguez, OCD. Washington DC: ISC Publications, 1979.

John of the Cross. *The Spiritual Canticle*. In *The Collected Works of St. John of the Cross*. Translated by Kieran Kavanaugh, OCD and Otilio Rodriguez, OCD. Washington DC: ISC Publications, 1979.

John of the Cross. *The Dark Night*. In *The Collected Works of St. John of the Cross*. Translated by Kieran Kavanaugh, OCD and Otilio Rodriguez, OCD.Washington DC: ISC Publications, 1979, 1991.

Keating, Thomas. "Psychology and the Spiritual Journey," *Contemplative Outreach News* (December 2006).

Merton, Thomas. *Thoughts in Solitude*. New York: Farrar, Straus and Giroux, 1956, rev. ed. 1984.

Merton, Thomas. *Thomas Merton: Disputed Questions*. New York: Harcourt Press, 1985.

Metz, Johannes Baptist. *Poverty of Spirit*. Translated by John Drury. New York: Paulist Press, 1968.

Mother Teresa of Calcutta. *Thirsting for God: Mother Teresa's Yearbook of Prayers, Meditations and Anecdotes for the Third Millennium*. Cincinnati: Servant Publications, 2000.

Mother Teresa of Calcutta. *Mother Teresa: Come Be My Light: The Private Writings of the Saint of Calcutta.* New York: Doubleday, 2007.
Stein, Edith. *The Science of the Cross.* Translated by Joseph Koeppelm, OCD. Washington DC: ICS Publications, 2003.
Teresa of Avila. *The Way of Perfection.* In *The Collected Works of St. Teresa of Avila.* Vol.2. Translated by Kieran Kavanaugh, OCD and Otilio Rodriguez, OCD. Washington DC: ISC Publications, 1980.
Thérèse of Lisieux. *Story of a Soul: The Autobiography of St. Thérèse of Lisieux,* 3d ed. Translated by John Clarke, OCD. Washington, DC: ICS Publications, 1996.

ABOUT THE AUTHOR

Barbara Hughes holds a Master's Degree in Formative Spirituality from Duquesne University and is additionally a registered nurse. She has worked in a variety of clinical settings and was employed by Catholic Charities of Eastern Virginia, where she served as the Director of Student Counseling, and later, as the Director of Family Life Education. She has worked in ministry on the parish and diocesan level for the Catholic Church. She currently authors a daily column on spirituality entitled "In Light of Faith" which has appeared in *The Catholic Virginian* since 2000. She was also a correspondent for the paper for five years.

She has been involved in interreligious dialogue since 2000. In 2007, she was appointed the Bishop's Liaison to the Jewish and Muslim communities for the Diocese of Richmond. A Secular Carmelite, wife, mother of five children, and a grandmother, she continues to lecture on spirituality, contemplative prayer and interreligious dialogue.